With Her LAST BREATH

"Of the many causes of death, suicide is uniquely disruptive to those left behind. Feelings of guilt, anger and grief pile on top of the deep sense of loss that family members and friends experience when a loved one takes their own life. Barb Roberts knows of all this both pastorally and personally. In this profoundly wise book she uses the heart-breaking story of her niece's suicide to provide help and hope for all who have been similarly wounded. I highly recommend *With Her Last Breath* as an oasis of comfort and insight to anyone navigating the tough times and difficult questions that the tragedy of suicide creates."

—**Scott Wenig**, Professor of Applied Theology, Haddon Robinson Chair of Biblical Preaching, Denver Seminary

"Barb Roberts is the most caring and gentle-spirited person that I have ever met. In a way that can only be called Christ-like, she quite simply helps those that hurt. When she speaks, I listen. When she writes, I read her words. Her openness in talking about her niece Kathy's journey, as gut wrenching of a subject as we face in society, is meant to help us all."

— **Brad Meuli**, Pres/CEO, Denver Rescue Mission

"The painful trauma of suicide is in the foreground of this deeply caring, biblically grounded guide to true compassion and real comfort. Barb Roberts covers a full range of grief and loss with wisdom and gifts nurtured over decades of serving as Director of Caring Ministries in a thriving church. Whether you are suffering loss or striving to love those who are, Barb's spiritual direction and practical insights will strengthen and guide you. From beginning to end this is a book about hope and comfort. If you believe people are not problems that need fixing; but image-bearers of God who, no matter how troubled and broken, need

God's saving love, you will resonate *With Her Last Breath* and share in Barb Roberts' passion to care for others."

—**Doug Webster**, Professor of Pastoral Theology. Beeson Divinity School, Birmingham, Alabama

"In *With Her Last Breath* Barb Roberts breathes new life into the complex but necessary conversation about suicide. With a rare look into the thoughts of one who reached the ultimate point of despair and took her own life, this book bravely treads into terrain few dare to publicly go. Out of a reservoir of personal anguish and hopeful faith, Barb Roberts walks with readers into and through the valley of the shadow of suicide with wisdom and grace. With rising tides of suicide in America, this is a timely and faithful book for individuals and Christian fellowships looking to better understand, more clearly see in advance, and more carefully engage those contemplating taking their last breath."

—**Carmen LaBerge**, Author, Director of Common Ground Christian Network, and host of Reconnect with Carmen and Connecting Faith

"I make my living teaching, caring, and teaching others to care. In this, I have worked alongside Barb Roberts for over twenty years. I know of no one who is better at shepherding people through loss and grief than Barb. She is the caring master. In everything she does, she adds wisdom and connects deeply with her heart. This book brings new depth and insights to the torn-up, gut-wrenching world of despair and death. God has gifted Barb to love people and see the truth when many others are losing their grip. Her perceptiveness into deep loss makes this book a must read for those who deal with the maddening expedition of suicide."

— **Dr. Brad Strait**, Senior Pastor, Cherry Creek Presbyterian Church, and Associate Professor in Spiritual Formation and Leadership, Denver Seminary.

According to the CDC, suicides in America are at their highest rate in 50 years. It is now the second leading cause of death for young people between ages 10 and 34. Which means that few families are left untouched by the tragic yet complicated stories that lead someone to take their own life. Barb Roberts' family was not. Neither was mine.

How does one even begin to process the pain, the loss, and the questions, let alone the risk factors and warning signs that accompany this unwanted journey?

Barb Roberts' first book was entitled *Helping Those Who Hurt*. Her new book could very well have been titled *Helping Those Who Have Been Touched by Suicide*. It is filled with raw realism, sustaining hope, and practical advice.

—**Don Sweeting**, President, Colorado Christian University

With Her
LAST BREATH

*A Tale of Suicide
and the Hope
of Heaven*

Barbara M. Roberts

NASHVILLE

NEW YORK • LONDON • MELBOURNE • VANCOUVER

With Her Last Breath
A Tale of Suicide and the Hope of Heaven

© 2020 **Barbara M. Roberts**

Published in New York, New York, by Morgan James Publishing. Morgan James is a trademark of Morgan James, LLC. www.MorganJamesPublishing.com

ISBN 978-1-64279-378-9 paperback
ISBN 978-1-64279-379-6 eBook
Library of Congress Control Number: 2018914141

Cover Design by:
Rachel Lopez
www.r2cdesign.com

Interior Design by:
Bonnie Bushman
The Whole Caboodle Graphic Design

In an effort to support local communities, raise awareness and funds, Morgan James Publishing donates a percentage of all book sales for the life of each book to Habitat for Humanity Peninsula and Greater Williamsburg.

Get involved today! Visit
www.MorganJamesBuilds.com

TABLE OF CONTENTS

PREFACE

Understanding what is going on in a person's mind just prior to the final decision to end their own life seems beyond our grasp. Often we are given information that attempts to explain the act of suicide; we are told of their depression, their pain, their grief. We are even at times made aware of the contents of what is referred to as the suicide note. The despair and finality involved when someone takes their life leaves those left behind grasping for information and answers. These thoughts ring true to me on a cognitive level as one who has been involved in pastoral care ministry since 1985; however, when the one who committed suicide was in our own family, the pain cut to a deeper level.

When I first heard that my niece, Kathy, had suicided, I couldn't believe it. The shock was so intense and devastating. If only; if only I had called her more often; if only we had taken her to dinner one more time; if only I had taken her suicide talk more seriously; if only I had found out what her plan was, maybe I could have stopped her. Perhaps I could have done something. I felt guilty and knew that I had not done enough.

Yet at the same time I knew all the "right" things. I knew someone could not stop another from taking his or her life. I knew I could not have rescued Kathy, nor can I rescue anyone else for that matter.

As I continue to grapple with Kathy's choice, I now have a different perspective of someone else's pain in the aftermath of a loved one's suicide. Being a pastoral caregiver does not exempt me from the same struggles others face. I empathize with their hurts and struggles.

It hurts to lose a family member at any time and under any circumstances; however, death by suicide is a unique and intensely devastating kind of grief tapping into the deep emotions of grief and guilt and anger and sadness. In the midst of such a deep loss, God promises never to go away, never to leave us nor forsake us. He is with us. He is God. He is with the person in despair and He is with the griever. I know God was with Kathy on that early morning, and though I believe she knew God was with her, she had set her mind to leave her difficult life and escape the pain in which she constantly found herself.

The pain of suicide while individual is also familial. Listen to these words from other survivors:

"I have relived the weeks before our son's suicide over and over again, wondering whether I could have prevented his death."

"All of her friends knew. She had talked to them about killing herself. They didn't believe her. None of them told me. I had no idea."

"I never realized my sister was so desperate. She was so good at covering up her real feelings."

There are those who would assert that despair and hope are mutually exclusive, as though one deals with either despair or hope. I believe, however, that many deal with despair intermingled with hope. Kathy wrote a 26 page journal which was found after her death. When I first read through Kathy's journal, I knew I was reading something that in more than three decades of pastoral ministry, I had never seen. There are many who upon making the decision to take their lives, choose to write a suicide note to explain their pain and heartache, to ask for forgiveness for what they are about to do, or perhaps to blame someone-even if that someone is them. However, I have not previously read such a complete journal that chronicles the hours just before her death (perhaps 36+ hours) leading up to the suicide, not only detailing the act itself but the reasoning behind. Her journal describes a lonely, hopeless life, explaining why she could not stay here on this earth one more day. Remarkably, through it all she did not lose sight of "the hope of Heaven." Kathy was confident that she would be there. Kathy experienced both despair and hope.

I've pondered the setting and the purposes of this book. Should it be to tell Kathy's family history? Should it be a guide for caregivers or for the hurting people themselves, showing a journal of pain mixed with hope and a real look at someone who struggles alone? It is important to remember that caregivers do not have to be only professionals, rather everyone has the potential to come alongside, to listen and to comfort one who is hurting.

I believe this book is multi-purpose:

- To share and understand Kathy's Journal
  o A glimpse into Kathy's life
  o Understanding that despair and hope are intermingled. One does not necessarily cancel the other. The pain and the hope are intertwined in the irregular and messy journey we call life.
- To help the weary Caregiver
  o Identify the signs
  o Practical ways to help
  o Telling the truth
  o Understanding a loving God by seeing His compassionate heart.

Perhaps it used to be a somewhat common opinion that Christians did not commit suicide. However, I have personally walked through this valley with a number of families and have even been aware of godly, hurting pastors who have taken their lives. We all know that any tragedy that happens in the secular world can happen in faith circles as well. This tragedy knows no bounds. It visits the houses of faithful Christians, law-abiding citizens, loving families, and veterans who are taking their lives at an alarming rate every day. There is no foolproof way to protect ourselves from this pain. How wonderful it would be if there were. Nevertheless, sometimes Christians seem more ashamed when a loved one commits suicide. It appears to be a personal affront to their beliefs and a statement of a lack of faith. But this generalization has no authenticity.

Listen in on one teen's thoughts: "The one thing that parents don't understand, and yet may be the biggest problem many young people face, is loneliness. Loneliness can go above and beyond struggling with some kind of addiction, or sex or drugs or alcohol or relationships or disappointments or loss. No matter how many friends, boyfriends or girlfriends, family members, or how strong a teen's faith is, the loneliness is right there. He or she can feel isolated even though there are thousands of others going through the exact same things. It is the loneliness and failure that can bring a lot of kids to the thought of suicide. Sometimes a teen thinks suicide is the answer because it is the end of the pain."

Pretty profound thoughts. How incredibly sad to hear a quote from one so young and to carry those thoughts to an end point, to think of a young person who lives to be only 14 or 15 or 16 or 17 or 18 years. What can be done about that loneliness, yours or someone else's? Who understands? We are told in the Bible, that we have a High Priest (Jesus) who understands all of our infirmities including our loneliness, not just some; not just when you are a little bit lonely; not just when you get cancer or have some major thing happen in your family. He understands all of our struggles. He understands all of our pain, all of our loneliness. "The Lord is close to the brokenhearted." Psalms 34:18. "Come to me, all you who are weary and burdened, and I will give you rest. Take my yoke upon you and learn from me, for I am gentle and humble in heart, and you will find rest for your souls. For my yoke is easy and my burden is light." Matthew 11:28. He does not say your burden is easy or that your burden is light. He lifts our load; He carries our burdens. If at any time our faith is going to make sense, be real, help us live our life, it is at a point of extreme loneliness.

Christians can have chemical imbalances that cause clinical depression just like anyone else. They can feel that life has no purpose and that the suffering is too great to endure for even one more day, just like anyone else. They can experience hopelessness, just like anyone else. One might ask the question, "Well, what about the phrase often quoted, God will never give you more than you can handle?" OK, let's look at what that verse really says, "God is faithful; he will not let you be tempted beyond what you can bear. But when you are tempted, he will also provide a way out so that you can stand up under it." I Corinthians 10:13. Often the Bible is taken out of context, and we are left trying to understand or explain something that is not accurately depicted. The context of that passage lets us know that God is faithful and will not leave us; that he will provide help in our temptations. Sometimes people do not use the way out that God provides but rather choose their own solution.

I read a phrase recently that still resonates deeply within me. This phrase was in the middle of a dialogue between two people. She knows that he is in a caring field where he sees much pain and suffering, and she empathizes with him: "It's hard to care that much and never have a guaranteed outcome." He responds with the comment: "It's hard to care that much. Period." Many wouldn't understand that comment, but for me it gives voice to a life given to caregiving. Caring is what I do and it is who I am. Early on it became evident that He had made me to care about others. "The Sovereign Lord has given me an instructed tongue, to know the word that sustains the weary. He wakens me morning by morning, wakens my ear to listen like one being taught." Isaiah 50:4 resonates deeply within me. In fact, the Bible says in the Psalms, "For you created my inmost being; you knit me together in my mother's womb." As God makes us and gifts us, and those gifts are given to encourage and support others, He also empowers us to use the gifts He has placed within us. In the same way that our thumb print is unique, so are we, creatures made by a loving Creator for the good of those He brings into our lives. I was born with God awareness, a strong awareness of Him. From the time I was very young, God was right before me, in what I thought about, in what I did, in who I was.

To resume Kathy's story, Kathy knew God. She knew Him first through the example of her Grandma, who read the Bible to her and sang songs about Jesus with her. Though Kathy departed from her faith during her teen and young adult years, later on she again read the Bible and she prayed. For Kathy life was always a struggle financially and relationally. For years before she took her life, her health was bad, albeit through many of her own choices. She developed lung and breathing issues.

Kathy became self-focused, and couldn't see beyond her crummy life and her run-down apartment and the oxygen tanks that she had to drag around. Her thinking near the end of her life did not go beyond her own small circle. Prior to these last days of isolation, she had reached out to others in her own way, though by that time she had isolated herself from many friendships. I see in hindsight, she tried to re-create the "happiness" she experienced in those early years of childhood, hoping and on a few occasions even suggesting that we get the whole family together for family dinners, which admittedly we did not do often enough. In much of her life she was a very giving person and yet in spite of her good intentions to help people or do something nice for friends and family, she became stuck.

My oldest son, Kirk, comforted me after learning of Kathy's death with this thought: "Mom, it isn't her death that is the tragedy; the tragedy occurred throughout her life. Now her tragic life is over and she is at peace." Kirk's words were very helpful to me in the process of grieving Kathy's life and her death.

Chapter 1
RECOGNIZING THE SIGNS

"I must put an end to this tonight.
I just really can't take any of this anymore."

1

I MUST PUT AN END TO THIS TONIGHT - I JUST REALLY CAN'T TAKE ANY OF THIS ANYMORE. I ONLY WANT TO GO AND BE WITH MY GRANDMA AGAIN. I JUST FOUND OUT LAST NIGHT THAT THERE ARE ALL KINDS OF THESE BUGS THAT LOOK LIKE TICKS WHICH HAVE INFESTED THIS COUCH. THE ONLY WAY TO GET RID OF THEM WILL BE TO THROW OUT THE COUCH AND I DON'T KNOW HOW TO ACCOMPLISH THAT. I THOUGHT IT WAS JUST A FEW AT FIRST, BUT THEY ARE STUCK INTO ALL THE NOOKS AND CRANNIES, THERE MUST BE HUNDREDS OF THEM. IF I COULD DRAG THE COUCH OUT MYSELF I'D DO IT RIGHT NOW. SO I HAVE BEEN SITTING HERE ALL DAY AND ALL NIGHT KILLING THEM A FEW AT A TIME AS THEY COME OUT AND TRY TO CRAWL ON ME, I DIDN'T NEED SOMETHING LIKE THIS ON TOP OF EVERYTHING ELSE. I CAN'T HELP BUT WONDER WHAT GOD WANTS FROM ME BECAUSE THERE IS ONLY SO MUCH A PERSON CAN TAKE. THEY'RE COMING OUT 3 AND 4 AT A TIME NOW AND I CAN'T HARDLY KEEP UP KILLING THEM. I JUST GAVE UP AND GOT OFF THE COUCH. I DON'T KNOW WHERE THESE CREATURES CAME FROM BUT I DON'T THINK THEY'VE BEEN HERE LONG, I DIDN'T SEE THEM UNTIL LAST NIGHT. HOW CAN THIS BE HAPPENING? IT JUST DROVE ME THAT MUCH CLOSER TO ENDING IT. IT'S 1:00 A.M NOW AND I CAN'T GO OUT TO DO IT UNTIL 3:30 OR SO, TO MAKE SURE NO ONE ELSE WILL BE AROUND. I'M GOING TO TAPE A NOTE TO MY SHIRT TO CALL UNCLE WALT, I DON'T KNOW HOW ANYBODY WOULD FIND OUT OTHERWISE. I WASN'T REALLY PLANNING ON DOING IT TONIGHT ALTHOUGH I

You have just read page 1 of Kathy's journal, in her own handwriting. Each chapter in this book corresponds to an actual page in her journal. This is the story of Kathy whose life here on earth ended far too soon.

Unfortunately and heartbreakingly, in our country and around the world there are multitudes of people who have prematurely ended their lives. In all of those lives there is a story, a story that is uniquely theirs to tell. Admittedly, many of those stories have been told. In the telling of Kathy's story, it is my heart's desire that the God who loved Kathy will become known to others who are hurting and despairing. Perhaps through her death, Kathy's God will be sought after. Many have said that it is only in the "telling of the story" and "telling the story" again that healing begins to occur. When we hear another's story of suffering, we then may be able to make a bit more sense out of our own.

Kathy, a woman who in many ways seemed much younger than her chronological age, chose not to wait for her appointed time to die but rather to hurry the process along. Kathy completed the plan and the process in the early morning hours of August 21, 2012. Kathy lived those last few years in a very small world. She was isolated and lonely.

Who was Kathy? I want you to see her from the viewpoint of some of her family members.

Here are a few life snapshots written by her brother:

"There are some things I can comment on with authority, there are some things I cannot. The difference is that period of time between when my family was intact (father, mother, older sister, younger brother) and then suddenly when it was not. There was a before, and there was an after. I was the youngest, thereby least impacted by any negative memories of those events. There are some things I can clearly testify to. We were a family once, and as children, loved. I know Father and Mother loved me and my Sister, because I remember them telling us so.

"*My older sister Kathryn was bossy, I remember that mostly. But protective, I also remember that. Having children of my own now, I see that is very human and normal, how could she be otherwise? She was nearly five years older than me, and that much older is almost like an adult. She probably felt the same. She certainly acted accordingly.*

"*I called her Sister; I don't remember why. But remember that she humored me mostly, and called me Brother in return. I have to this day an impression of satire in her voice. I remember her discipline; funny I don't remember my mother's. I certainly remember my father's. I cannot say if there was direction to Kathryn from our parents to "watch out and take care of your little brother," or if it was self-initiated on her part or a need to exert control. Perhaps a task she was not either ready or able to perform, in the collapsed world she had to face at a critical young age.*

"*Then the Great Void. One minute we were a family, the next we were not. One minute Dad was there, the next minute he was a visitor in his own home. The divorce papers say "1968," that much I know. The effects on Kathryn can only be surmised. She took her own life in August of 2012, and cannot provide any answers for us. But we have some clues.*

"*I'm not certain when Kathryn left our broken home the first time; she was there at first, after our dad left. We were together for visits with Dad, often for whole weekends. I wasn't too young to notice changes though. Predominantly Mom and Kathryn were always-and I mean always-in a seemingly perpetual state of conflict; like a cascade, starting small and continuing to build incessantly over time. I remember thinking that kind of thing never happened before when Dad was around. I suppose next would be the time I discovered she started secretly smoking cigarettes. She "urged" me (I don't remember "threatened," never felt threatened by my sister) not to tell Mom. I complied; I always did, except for later on. I suppose the other big change that left an indelible memory was realizing around this time that her "friends" were not like the normal friends. They were different; not only Mom, but seemingly other adults not approving.*

"When she left our home, I cannot say with precision. But she was gone. It exasperates me to this day, that there is a Great Void of knowledge between what was and what came to be, a gap of first-hand testimony that might provide any context for the events that would transpire some forty-five years later. How can I remember so clearly what our family was about when I was four or five years old, but not between then and say eight or nine? One fact is clear: the relationship between Kathryn and our mother died. She went to live with our Dad, I subsequently learned later though there were no additional details. I have very little first-hand knowledge of those critical two to three years. What transpired in those years is unknown to me. But I was nevertheless relieved that the strife in our home was eliminated, and at least our Mom and I could get on with life. However, after a while she was back. No reason given, just more rebellion as the order of the day, constant turmoil, endless conflict, hostility and tension. It was here I began to grasp the true meaning of a broken family and broken people. We were not the same as others, we were not right. We were wrong; this was wrong. Seems like it was always wrong, with Kathryn around. At least that's what I remember.

"That would always be a factor for my sister until her dying day. The only thing she desperately wanted, long into her turbulent adult years and even to the very end, was reconciliation and relationship with our mother. Only at the end did she realize that it takes two people to make a real relationship; as hard as you might

want the relationship, there has to be a similar assent by the other. Sadly, that never happened.

"Then Kathryn began to trust Jesus in a new way. It was late enough in life for her not to have the opportunity for significant spiritual growth and maturity, but enough to know where she was going and who would take her there. Somewhere between the Prodigal Child and the Thief on the Cross, that was her path. And enough to know that what she was leaving behind was not worthy to be compared to the glory that would be revealed in her. She instinctively understood and fled to His heart.

"I cast no judgment on my Sister's decision to take her own life. I wish she had acted differently, just as I wish her life on the earth had been different. I wish that she had not had to bear what no young girl should have to bear in the destruction of her family, or the destruction of her body through acts of her own negligence. She was, like every one of us, designed otherwise.

"In Kathryn's letter, written during her final 36 hours as she contemplated suicide before committing the final act, she makes an ominous declaration: that she knew she was loved as a child, had essentially spent all she had in mind, soul, and body on the earth trying to recapture that in various ways, and finally realizing that her salvation in all things was only in the Lord who loves without limit or reservation, and gave Himself for her personally. In the end, her desire to be with her Lord essentially far exceeded her ability to endure life in its present form here."

And words from her two uncles:

"She was bright, happy and delightful, and as a confident 5 year old, she once corrected an adult on the plural of the word hippopotamus; "it's hippopotami." Often left alone at home by two working parents,

and eventually by a single mom, Kathy assumed the role of daytime mother to her brother, 5 years her junior. The "happy" home and intact marriage disintegrated, and she increasingly struggled with relationships. After high school she joined the Air Force, drifted into a life style which further strained the relationship with her mother and stepfather. She became a heavy smoker, and adopted a life of alcohol and even drugs.

"Kathy's attempts to bring her partner home with her were refused by her mother, thus further straining that relationship. She frequently borrowed money from her parents, loans which were seldom paid back, which all but destroyed those bonds.

"After the Air Force, Kathy began to drift through life alone, not quite comfortable with her life style, but never fitting in with other relationships. She was mostly alone. She landed a job with a large defense contractor as a welder. Emotional problems worsened and interfered with her job performance and she eventually lost her job. She lived on disability insurance and Social Security.

"After her grandmother died, Kathy moved into her grandmother's house. The young married couple living in the small basement apartment of that house found the situation intolerable and soon moved out which eliminated part of Kathy's monthly income. Kathy could not afford the house on her meager disability and social security income alone and she had to move out as well. There were several attempts by relatives and a neighbor to "take her in", but Kathy continued to struggle with relationships and ended up burning most of her bridges. Those folks loved her, but couldn't live with her.

"After staying with an uncle and then other friends briefly, she moved into a small apartment by herself. She probably was still heavily self-medicating, which left her sluggish and sleepy. One day having dozed off while smoking, a fire erupted in her apartment.

She was burned, and this added to the lung damage already caused by heavy smoking. Eventually this led to her ongoing need to carry around an oxygen tank. While we had thought that things couldn't get worse for her, life dropped to a new low point.

"Following that difficult period, she seemed to make a turnaround, desirous of following the Lord and wanting to have a good working relationship with people. But old patterns were difficult to break, and there remained a tendency for manipulation and scheming, appearing cooperative while still living life in her own self-centered way. Basically she quit living, but at the same time needed others to take care of her basic needs.

"There was one person, Lorene, in Kathy's life who somehow managed to become an anchor for her. Lorene was the girlfriend of Kathy's father who had died several years earlier. While Kathy lived alone, this lady became her main support system. However, a serious illness suddenly claimed the life of this dear lady, leaving Kathy adrift in an otherwise dreary and lonely life. Lorene's death was another final straw. For those looking on, it was obvious that this was very difficult for Kathy to deal with; but I don't believe any of us understood how fatal a blow this death really was. Lorene was one of her life-lines. She was her transportation and her encourager. She became ill very suddenly, which she kept hidden from Kathy, and was soon gone. For a person teetering on the brink, yet one more loss can be devastating. Somewhere in the midst of that latest loss, she made the decision to end her life.

"And those of us left behind grieve."

When People Grieve

When people are grieving, they go through many different stages and experience a wide range of emotions. Emotions which are closely associated with grief include; shock, denial, guilt, depression, anger, anxiety and fear. The stages are at times difficult to name. In fact, sometimes when I am just generally ticked, and I can't figure out why, the red flag to me is "what am I grieving?" What loss am I experiencing, because anger is a part of grieving. It is interesting that we can experience to varying degrees many of these emotions— from relatively short-term issues of grief and loss, to the pain of losing someone loved.

For the family who has discovered their loved one has taken his or her life, there often are immediate and sometimes long-lasting effects.

Many of the painful parts of the process of grief in death by suicide are similar to other deaths. Emotions that range from crying and shock to nightmares, confusion, loss of sleep and appetite. There often is a need to review and focus on events leading up to the death, even to idealize the one who died, repeatedly contemplating the events leading up to the death or loss.

Several factors can put any person at risk for suicide.

Risk factors of suicide include:
- History of previous suicide attempts.
- Family history of suicide.
- History of depression or other mental illness.
- Alcohol or drug abuse.
- Stressful life event or loss.
- Easy access to lethal methods.
- Exposure to the suicidal behavior of others.
- Incarceration.

Warning Signs of Suicide:
- Talks about committing suicide.
- Suddenly has trouble eating or sleeping and is despondent, with little interest in life.

- Experiences drastic changes in behavior, such as losing all interest in things that have previously been important like hobbies, work, or school.
- Withdrawal from friends and social activities.
- Prepares for death by making out a will or funeral arrangements, gets affairs in order, contacts family members and friends to tell them he or she loves them in ways that seem to be saying good-bye.
- Gives away prized possessions.
- Has attempted suicide before.
- Experiencing recent and severe losses, especially a suicide by someone close.
- Is preoccupied with death and dying.
- Loses interest in personal appearance.
- Dramatically increases use of drugs and alcohol.
- Suddenly appears euphoric, after having been depressed. (Once the decision is made to commit suicide, the person may feel resolute in following through with the plan, and his/her demeanor changes.)

Many behavioral and verbal clues (some subtle, others more obvious) can alert a parent, spouse, teacher, counselor or friend to one's suicidal intentions. A person at risk of committing suicide may be experiencing deep depression, which may be indicated by loss of weight, appetite or interest in personal appearance, change in sleeping patterns, fatigue, feelings of hopelessness and low self-esteem. Sudden behavioral changes may occur: the person may become disruptive, violent, or hostile toward family and friends; or inexplicably moody, suspicious, anxious, or selfish. He or she may spend a great deal of time daydreaming, fantasizing, or imagining ills, in extreme cases experiencing memory lapses or hallucinations.

Chapter 2
GRIEVING AND SUICIDE

"Just Plain Tired. I'm so tired of everything being so hard."

KNEW IT WOULD BE SOON. BUT THE BUGS ARE REALLY THE LAST STRAW. THERE IS ONLY SO MUCH I CAN TAKE, I ONLY HAVE SO MUCH FIGHT IN ME AND NO MORE. I'M SO TIRED OF EVERYTHING BEING SO HARD. I OFTEN WONDER WHAT I DID TO DESERVE THIS END. I MAY NOT BE THE BEST PERSON BUT I ALWAYS TRIED TO BE A GOOD PERSON. I WISH I DIDN'T HAVE TO LEAVE MY PLACE IN SUCH A MESS, BUT EVEN IF I CLEANED FOR THE NEXT 12 HOURS IT WOULD ONLY MAKE A DENT. IT DOESN'T MATTER TO ME WHAT HAPPENS TO ANY OF THIS STUFF, AS LONG AS SCOTT GETS THE PHOTOGRAPHS AND MY GRANDMOTHER'S BRACELET. I'M SORRY THAT IT WILL BE LEFT TO UNCLE WALT TO DEAL WITH EVERYTHING — IT WOULD HAVE BEEN LORENE, BUT SHE HAD TO LEAVE BEFORE ME.

ANOTHER DAY AND I FEEL LIKE I AM IN A LIVING HELL — NOBODY KNOWS HOW HARD IT HAS BECOME JUST TO EXIST. I KNOW THAT THERE'S ONLY ONE WAY TO END THIS BUT I HAVEN'T BEEN ABLE TO BRING MYSELF TO DO IT YET — MAYBE TONIGHT. I WOKE UP THIS AFTERNOON AFTER HARDLY SLEEPING AT ALL. I TRIED TO GO BACK TO SLEEP SO I DIDN'T HAVE TO FACE THIS DAY BUT IT'S TOO HOT. I AM SITTING EVER SO GENTLY ON THE COUCH SO AS NOT TO DISTURB THE BUGS. I DON'T KNOW WHY GOD IS PUTTING ME THROUGH THIS, IT WAS HARD ENOUGH BEFORE BUT NOW IT'S PRACTICALLY UNBEARABLE. I CAN'T HARDLY BREATHE FOR THE LAST COUPLE OF DAYS. I NEED TO TAKE A BATH AND CHANGE CLOTHES BUT I CAN'T BECAUSE I CAN'T HARDLY BREATHE. I JUST GOT A CALL THAT I HAVE A DOCTOR'S APPOINTMENT ON MONDAY, EVEN IF I WANTED TO GO,

Some signals should come through loud and clear: he/she may express a desire to die, threaten to commit suicide, or inform friends of a plan. For a teen, self-abusive acts such as cutting and self-inflicting cigarette burns are potential suicidal gestures.

Do any of the above-signs fit you? Get help. Find someone to talk to.

But what if you are the Caregiver? What do you do?

- Be non-judgmental.
- Treat your friend's problems seriously.
- Take all threats seriously.
- Do not try to talk the person out of it.
- Ask direct questions, such as, "Have you been thinking of killing yourself?"
- Communicate your concern and support.
- Offer yourself as a caring listener until professional help can be arranged.
- Try to assess the seriousness of the risk, to make the appropriate referral to a health care professional, counselor, or concerned teacher.
- Do not agree to be sworn to secrecy. Contact someone who can help your friend if he or she will not make the contact personally.
- Do not leave the person alone if you feel the threat is immediate.
- Take all plans and threats seriously (even if you suspect this is "merely a plea for attention"). You cannot take the risk that you may be wrong.
- If you get a response that in any way appears that this is a possibility, your next question should be, "Have you thought what that might look like? How might you harm yourself?"

- The next important question is to find out, do they have the means to complete the plan?
- Then get help. Better to have them mad than dead.
- Don't ignore.
- Don't minimize.

As I think of many specific examples of troubled individuals who have taken their lives, there are struggles that are common to each one; intense grief and loss, hopelessness, what seems like to them a good solution to a situation they can endure no longer.

In my years of ministry experience, there are many personal examples. Some that come to mind include:

- the young husband who had abuse in his past,
- the five teens who couldn't handle the pain any longer,
- the young wife who suffered from a mental disorder,
- the Dad in ministry who had a disabled daughter,
- the young Mom living an affluent life yet struggling with depression,
- the teen who had just returned from a church youth retreat only to take his Dad's gun and shoot himself.

All of them were hurting, felt hopeless, were lonely and would not believe that help was available.

Recognizing that someone is in need of help and sensing we could be involved in helping are only part of the story. Sometimes we who want to be a caregiver feel we cannot take on anybody else's trouble because we are overwhelmed with our own. Perhaps one of the most challenging growth areas for each of us as caregivers, is to understand selflessness—being a servant.

Chapter 3
SERVING THE LONELY

"How Did I Ever Wind up So Alone"

3

I can't so I'll have to cancel it. I am trying to trust God like Uncle Walt said, but every day is worse than the day before. Killing myself is the only thing that makes any sense to me. Nothing seems to matter to me except letting go of this impossible life - how did it ever get to be this bad? How did I ever wind up so alone? I know that God is with me all the time and because of that I shouldn't have any fear, but I am full of it. The only thing that's keeping me from completely losing my mind at this moment is writing it all down. I just found a bug crawling across my shirt, it's not safe to sit here. I really can't deal with any of this anymore, I've finally had enough. I wish I didn't have to spend the last hours of my life alone and worrying about bugs crawling all over me, I can't even try to relax on the couch. I could spend this time reflecting my life, but there's not really much to look at - I have a ton of regrets. I wish I could believe that my life has counted for something but I just can't see it. It seems only a small accumulation of things and no more well, I can't sit on the couch for the duration, the bugs are everywhere. Why has this happened on top of everything else? I could have gone my whole life without a problem like this and been happy! All of this is pointing me in one direction, up to the balcony and over the edge. I welcome it, I don't know why it has to be so hard to do. I can't think of anything better than being with Grandma again in Heaven, except for meeting Jesus face to face. I can only

Understanding Servanthood

In Christ's day, the roads throughout Palestine were dry and dusty. When the rains came, they turned into seas of mud. As travelers walked along these roads, their feet and sandals became dirty. Can you envision as the disciples gathered, they may have had an inner struggle—knowing the right thing to do and yet being human like you and me. "I wonder who's going to be the one to stoop (literally) and wash those dirty feet. I hope no one expects it to be me. My back hurts, my knees lock when I stoop like that, they may have cuts on their feet and long, dirty toenails that make the job disgusting. I hope the homeowner has a servant there to wash our feet. I'd like to have my feet washed first so that the towel isn't too soiled or the water too dirty."

Those might be our reactions if we were truly honest, but Jesus' call to us is a higher one. In fact, He personified for us for all eternity what it means to truly wash one another's feet. He could have just told us how important it was to Him that we serve one another; He could have explained the spiritual and cultural significance of wiping the dirty feet of one another, but instead He actually demonstrated in a very clear, obvious way what it means to be a servant. He took on the garment of a servant and washed His disciples' feet and tells us to do likewise. Have you ever washed another's feet by participating in a foot-washing ceremony? Or, more importantly, have you had someone wash your feet? It's a very humbling experience. For those who are struggling, even despairing, having someone serve *them* might be the one thing in their hopeless world that gives them hope.

What other servant symbols might be used in your own family, in your neighborhood, at your office, in your friend group to exemplify to another that you want to wash their feet? Might you bite your tongue when you want to take credit for something; might you listen to someone's story yet again when you have heard it numerous times before; might you let them shine rather than yourself; might you go to their home and help with projects when you sense they are weary and over-whelmed while knowing that you have projects of your own that need to be tackled? What about being a shoulder to cry on, or an ear to listen, or a ride to the attorney's office when they'd rather not go alone?

Jesus knew what was ahead. Jesus not only loved His followers, He showed them the full extent of that love. Jesus understood the power God had put in His hands. So, realizing all of the above He chose to remove His outer clothing, take on the garment of a servant and perform a servant act. This was not for show, not just a cursory act as the leader to show them how to do it and then letting them do the rest. He genuinely wanted to show them His love for them as individuals with dirty feet. But He also did not miss the opportunity to talk through the example. This was not just a lesson in foot washing but a demonstration of love in action and a teaching tool for His disciples. There is no doubt that this is a pass-on-able lesson. He told them, not in parables but directly, I want you to do this, too. He promises a blessing to those who follow His example. "But just as you excel in everything—in faith, in speech, in knowledge, in complete earnestness and in your love for us—see that you also excel in this grace of giving." II Corinthians 8:7. These gifts are rather intangible, not necessarily the ones you wrap in a box with beautiful paper and tie with an imaginative bow, but rather the gift of yourself. Sometimes what another needs is not just the thing we buy for them or do for them or say to them, but us.

We can present:

- The gift of undivided attention, being fully present, putting down something you are working on and taking up their need, their cause, and their concern.
- The gift of serving. Being a servant. It has been said, "You'll know you have the heart of a servant by how you respond when you are treated like one." Does serving come easy for

you? If you are like me, the answer is yes and no. Some days and sometimes it is easy for me; others, not so much.

- The gift of noticing, being aware of someone's struggles.
- The gift of prayer, praying with and praying for. Asking for specific things to pray about.
- The gift of grace. The same un-deserved love and care that God lavishes upon us.
- The gift of time, no matter how busy. Nothing is more important than giving of yourself and your time.

Chapter 4
THE PAIN IS TOO BAD

"I can only imagine that Heaven is a million times better than here."

4

IMAGINE THAT HEAVEN IS A MILLION TIMES BETTER THAN HERE. THERE IS NO BETTER PLACE TO BE. NO MORE TEARS OR SORROW OF ANY KIND, ONLY JOY AND PEACE. WHY WOULDN'T ANYONE WANT TO GO TO HEAVEN AS SOON AS POSSIBLE? IT MAKES ME WONDER WHY I'VE WAITED SO LONG TO GET TO THIS POINT. STILL, IT'S GOING TO BE HARD TO MAKE MYSELF GO UP THE STAIRS AND ACTUALLY DO IT. EVEN AT THIS MOMENT I'M NOT SURE IF I HAVE THE NERVE. BUT I KNOW IT'S THE ONLY WAY, THE ONLY THING THAT MAKES ANY SENSE TO ME. IT'S NOW 10 MORE HOURS UNTIL 3:30 A.M. — THAT WILL BE THE BEST TIME WHEN HOPEFULLY NO ONE WILL BE AROUND. I CAN'T STOP THINKING ABOUT LORENE AND HOW, NEXT TO GRANDMA SHE'S THE FIRST PERSON I'D LIKE TO MEET IN HEAVEN. I NEVER GOT TO SAY GOODBYE AND IT WILL BE SO GOOD TO SEE HER AGAIN, I'VE MISSED HER SO MUCH. HER DAUGHTERS DON'T KNOW HOW MUCH I LOVED HER AND IT SHOWS IN THE WAY THEY'VE TREATED ME. I KNOW IT'S BEEN HARD ON THEM, BUT IT'S BEEN REALLY HARD FOR ME TOO AND MY FEELINGS DON'T SEEM TO MATTER. I WISH I COULD ASK GOD TO HELP ME KILL MYSELF BUT THAT WOULDN'T BE RIGHT. I KNOW I'M GOING AGAINST HIS WILL FOR ME AND THAT BOTHERS ME A LOT, BUT I JUST CAN'T GO ON THIS WAY NOT EVEN FOR ANOTHER DAY. I WISH I WAS DEAD ALREADY SO I WOULDN'T HAVE TO GO THROUGH THE TROUBLE OF CLIMBING THE STAIRS, TYING THE ROPE AND LETTING MYSELF DROP. IT SOUNDS SO EASY BUT IT'S GOING TO TAKE A LOT OF EFFORT. THE LETTING GO WILL BE THE HARDEST PART. MY HEAD IS SWIMMING, I'M GOING TO LAY BACK DOWN FOR A FEW MINUTES.

I JUST TOOK A SHOWER AND 3 BUGS CAME CRAWLING

Kathy's story needs to be told, and particularly her end-of-life journal needs to be read, not just to make sense out of her life or her premature death, but because it can help. Help those who are hurting and despairing and desirous of another path—another answer, another to understand their pain.

We read page after page of pain in Kathy's journal. But now, she is no longer just imagining what it is like to be in God's very presence; she is there. She had been in pain for years, physical pain certainly, but more intense was the emotional pain and the rejection that she felt. It was difficult to know how best to care for her in her pain.

Chapter 5
YOUR WORLD IS ROCKED

*"Try as I have, I can only come up
with good reasons to check out."*

OUT OF MY SHIRT - THERE IS NO HOPE. I HAVE TO DO IT TONIGHT, THERE ISN'T ANY REASON FOR WAITING ANYMORE. THE BUGS REALLY ARE THE LAST STRAW. I WONDER HOW MANY WILL COME CRAWLING OUT WHEN THEY CUT ME DOWN. I WISH I COULD FIND ONE GOOD REASON TO STAY, A REASON TO CHOOSE LIFE - BUT TRY AS I HAVE, I CAN ONLY COME UP WITH GOOD REASONS TO CHECK OUT NOW. I WAS THINKING YESTERDAY ABOUT MY MOTHER AND HOW SHE MIGHT REACT TO FINDING OUT THAT I KILLED MYSELF, I DON'T IMAGINE IT WILL MAKE ANY DIFFERENCE TO HER AT ALL. STILL, I THINK IT'S SAD THAT WE NEVER GOT TO TALK ABOUT THINGS, BUT IT WAS HER CHOICE TO REMOVE ME AND SCOTT FROM HER LIFE. THE THING IS, I HAVEN'T EVER UNDERSTOOD EXACTLY WHY. FOR A LONG TIME I THOUGHT IT WAS BECAUSE I USED TO BE GAY, BUT SCOTT HAS A PERFECT LIFE AND SHE DOESN'T WANT TO KNOW HIM EITHER. I CAN'T UNDERSTAND WHY SHE WOULDN'T WANT TO KNOW THE ONLY OTHER GRANDCHILD SHE'LL EVER HAVE, BUT SHE'S NEVER SENT KENZIE SO MUCH AS A BIRTHDAY CARD. WHAT DID EITHER OF US EVER DO TO CAUSE HER NOT TO LOVE US? I NEVER STOPPED LOVING HER - EVEN NOW, THERE'S NOTHING I WOULDN'T DO FOR HER IF I COULD. WHAT A WASTE!

IT WAS A REALLY STUPID REASON WHY I TOOK A SHOWER, I DON'T WANT THEM FINDING ME WITHOUT CLEAN CLOTHES AND HAIR. HOW VAIN CAN A PERSON GET? I ALSO WANTED JUST TO SEE IF I COULD ACTUALLY ACCOMPLISH A SHOWER - I ASKED FOR GOD'S HELP AND TOGETHER WE PULLED IT OFF. SOME PEOPLE MAY WONDER WHY THE BIG PRODUCTION OFF

Coping with Grief, Death by Suicide and Other Deaths

How does one cope with the suicide of a loved one? There is help available; there are tools and explanations. We have seen some of those tools and warning signs, but really, when all the tools and advice are given, there is raw pain, a gaping wound, a huge hole through which come the unhelpful voices loud and clear. "We didn't do enough." "We should have known." "We could have taken steps."

While death by suicide leaves in its wake complicated grief, there are components of the grieving similar to any other death. For the Christian watching their loved one die, there may be a bitter-sweet aura surrounding this very difficult time. Bitter because their loved one is dying, will be leaving, will no longer be here with them, will no longer be available for phone conversations, dinners, advice, hugs, and many other day-to-day touches of love. Sweet because that loved one will no longer be in pain, will be whole again, will be in the presence of our Lord.

We have talked about those who experience the grief of the death of their loved one. What about the grief experienced by the one who is dying?

Though family members may surround the bed of the dying, may keep a 24x7 vigil, may constantly minister to the needs of the dying, there can be a sense on the part of the dying that "I must do this alone; I am on my own; no human being can walk this valley with me." It can be a lonely valley. How critical, therefore, for that dying person to grasp Psalm 23, "Yea though I walk through the valley of the shadow of death, I need not fear evil, for He walks beside me; He will never leave me nor forsake me." God is there and here and around me and with me and in me. He is with me on this side; He will walk me through the valley; He will be with me on the other side.

He moves into our lonely, distorted, painful, confusing world with His gentle presence, usually in the persons of people who are there to give support, in whatever ways they can. God uses people to bring His presence into our broken world, either person to person, through notes, phone calls or emails—or a variety of other ways and means.

But for the one who is choosing to end his life, he may not appreciate or may not even be aware of the one God sends to help. He experiences that one final straw, the one additional stress, one more part of the thinking process that says "no more." The young Dad who feels like a failure; the teen who heard one more time what a loser he was; the housewife who has dealt with depression year after year and decides "that is enough," the senior who feels his dignity has been stripped from him one time too many; the businessman who loses his job. Though there may have been clues, (as in the case of Kathy, her words at times seemed hopeless), there is still in us the thought, if not really a conviction, "surely she doesn't mean it; certainly she will not actually act on the plan."

It seems reasonable and not at all unusual for the loved one to back away from the person who is talking about suicide, thinking perhaps if we just don't concentrate on the subject or even talk about it, he or she will forget and tomorrow will be a better day. However, entering into a dialogue with the one who expresses suicidal thoughts does not cause the person to end their life. It is at these times that the caregiver needs to recognize that there is a God who cares about the suicidal person and about us the caregiver as well. God is able to give wisdom to the one on the sideline and lead that person to give help and guidance for the struggler. The help lines are not only for the suicidal person, but for the one standing in the role of caregiver, knowing what steps to take next, where to turn, how to refer.

It is obviously best to involve the desperate person in the plan to refer, even if it makes them angry. It is better to have the person mad at you than to have them dead. Tell the person that you would really like to have them get the available help; however, also let them know that if they do not choose to get help, you will contact help for them.

Suicide is one of the least understood tragedies. Every so often a rash of suicides causes articles to be written, attention to be given, and help to be publicized. Then the crisis and the trauma and the attention go back into the closet until the family or individual or church or school has to deal with this tragedy again, leaving those who suffer to do it alone and in private.

What are some things you might do in a crisis to help a Kathy in your life?

- Pray. From the moment you learn of the crisis, recognize that it is as Scripture says, "not by might; nor by power; but by His Spirit" that anything will be accomplished through us.
- Demonstrate calmness, concern and acceptance and find out about the situation, being very intentional and loving in coming alongside.
- Listen long and hard and without interrupting. Either on the phone or in person be willing just to be, realizing that the person in crisis needs to tell their story.
- Let your demeanor be appropriate. This is a judgment call, but make sure that you are not pushy, or condescending or judgmental.
- Allow emotions to surface. Some people are uncomfortable with others' tears or anger. Recognize your difficulties in this area, realizing that the person in crisis *will* be emotional and needs a place to express it.
- When several people are involved in the crisis, deal with the most anxious or the key person first. A good example of this: in a hospital intensive care waiting room, discern which person needs you immediately.
- Remember that people in crisis are very often vulnerable. You are not there to fix their problem. You are there to support and

come alongside and your answer may not be the best one for them.

- Help the person in need identify others in their life who might be willing to help. It is important, when possible, to have more than one person helping through the crisis, and even more helpful to have the person in crisis identify those who could help. You may want to offer to contact those individuals.

- Ask if you can pray with the person in crisis. If yes, pray with them, not just for them.

- Share scripture when appropriate. Be very sensitive not to force Scripture upon someone in a crisis. Use your common sense. If it doesn't seem right to you to share, don't.

- It is most helpful for the crisis intervener to either be a resource or find resources for the one in pain. Your caring presence is, in fact, the caring presence of Christ.

- Give the person permission to grieve. The person needs someone to help them know that it is okay to be sad, and it is okay to be angry. It is even okay to cry or rage.

- The severity of the crisis depends upon numerous things: other issues going on concurrently, the perception of what this crisis might mean for their life, and their support network or lack thereof.

- Help the person be safe, particularly when you sense they are in danger of harming themselves or others.

- Be confidential. While you may need to involve others to help, it is imperative that the hurting person understand that you are a safe place.

- Recognizing your own limits of time and personal responsibilities, be available as needed or as often as possible.

As you continue to read through Kathy's journal, you will read of her struggles through the last hours of her life. Her thoughts are not the rantings of an angry, bitter woman at the end of a difficult life. They are very obviously heart-felt thoughts of pain and loneliness, despair and discouragement, the hope for a better place and a better day, and the spirit of forgiveness and being forgiven by a God whom she knows loves her and a God she hopes will understand her sorrow and despair.

Standing beside the bed or sitting on the bed of the one who is suffering is only part of the picture. I have often walked alongside of the sufferer for many years, and have often asked God to help me view them with His eyes, to see that individual as precious in God's sight, and in need of love and care.

Because God knows the intents and hidden places in the heart of the sufferer, He also knows our pain and discomfort as the caregiver. It is with His strength and His wisdom that we can sit beside the bed, recognizing that His power is made perfect in our weakness. It pleases Him to help us to see that person with His eyes and with His unconditional love. Their life choices may not be our own, their behavior may not be what we would choose, but our assignment as a caregiver is to be fully present with their pain and their suffering.

Chapter 6
GIVING CARE TO THE HURTING

*"Hanging myself. It's just a question of what
will work. I have to go with what I have, a rope."*

6

HANGING MYSELF. IT'S JUST A QUESTION OF WHAT WILL WORK. I'D RATHER HAVE A BOTTLE OF NARCOTICS OR A GUN, BUT I HAVE TO GO WITH WHAT I HAVE, A ROPE. I HAVE RAZOR BLADES BUT I'VE ALREADY TRIED THAT AND I JUST CAN'T MAKE MYSELF MAKE THE CUT, IT WOULD HURT TOO MUCH. ONCE I TRIED GETTING DRUNK TO DO IT BUT THAT ONLY MADE ME SO EMOTIONAL THAT I COULDN'T GO THROUGH WITH IT. THE ONLY WAY TO DO IT IS TO REMAIN DETACHED, IT HAS TO BE ALMOST LIKE SLEEPWALKING. I SOUND LIKE I'M SOME KIND OF SUICIDE EXPERT — HOW CAN ANYONE KNOW, YOU CAN ONLY KILL YOURSELF ONCE. I WON'T REALLY KNOW UNTIL I ACTUALLY LET GO. ENOUGH ABOUT THAT, IT'S SIMPLY A MATTER OF JUST DOING IT, NOTHING MORE.

WELL, I DIDN'T GO OFF THE BALCONY THIS MORNING. I WAITED TOO LONG AS I VACILLATED BETWEEN DOING IT THIS MORNING OR TOMORROW MORNING AND IT GOT TO BE TOO LATE — I THOUGHT SOMEONE MIGHT BE COMING OUT SOON TO GO TO WORK. IT NEEDS TO BE SOMETIME BETWEEN 3 AND 4 SO THAT I WILL HOPEFULLY HAVE COMPLETE PRIVACY. I SAY I COULDN'T DECIDE ABOUT IT, BUT THE TRUTH IS THAT I CHICKENED OUT. I WAS SUDDENLY AFRAID OF DYING. I DON'T THINK I AM NOW THOUGH, ALL I HAVE TO DO IS LOOK AT THE ALTERNATIVE, I'M PAYING FOR WAITING BY HAVING TO SPEND ANOTHER DAY IN THIS HELL OF AN EXISTENCE. I DIDN'T TURN ON THE T.V. ALL DAY YESTERDAY, AND SO FAR TODAY, BUT IT'S ONLY NOON AND THERE'S ONLY SO MUCH I

There is yet another piece of caring for the hurting. What if you are the one struggling and in pain, physical or emotional, and it is you in need of being cared for? How do you respond and allow others to care for you?

There are those who neither seek nor accept care, but others are willing to be cared for like my friend who recently died of ALS. She and her husband faced her disease with honesty and dignity. Others facing her devastating illness might have chosen suicide, but she was a beautiful sufferer who was patient and kind and loving. She had a great sense of humor, though for the last number of months of her life was unable to speak. I know she got frustrated and emotional, and every time I prayed with her, she cried, yet she and her husband had a peace that came from knowing that God walked beside them through it all.

Your world has been rocked. Maybe you are in the process of declaring bankruptcy. Your boss has just told you your job is being eliminated. You thought your marriage though not great, was okay, and now your spouse just said that he/she is unhappy and wants out of the relationship. This morning your daughter admitted to an eating disorder. Your son has been expelled from college. These situations have the potential to strip you of peace and stability and leave you feeling hopeless and in need of being cared for.

Maybe you have been the strong one, the listener, the helper, the caregiver, the one who prays. Maybe you find it can be difficult to be on the receiving end of care. In fact, a wise woman once said to me, "You know that phrase, "It's more blessed to give than to receive"? It's also a whole lot easier." Many of us know how to give care but have a difficult time receiving it.

We have looked at receiving care. Let us continue on with our look at those whose life ends very tragically. Two very different stories, Mark and Linda; very different lives; very different deaths. One died accidentally, the other by her own hand. Both were believers:

Linda was a woman of the Bible, but struggled with depression for many years; Mark was addicted to cocaine but had turned to Jesus a few weeks before his death. Mark was not quite able to accept the new-found freedom he had been given when he turned his life over to Jesus.

On a Friday afternoon, my family and I sat in a beautiful park attending a Memorial Service for Mark who was 42 years old and had been addicted to drugs since he was a teenager. He had been incarcerated; he had been involved in many fights; he had a young daughter. He had been a bright young teen but his addictions had taken over his life. He had just completed a six-year prison sentence. His had been a difficult life of addiction and imprisonment and fighting and hardship. A number of years before his death, he had been assigned a one-on-one Christian caregiver; however, shortly before his death he admitted that he really had not been ready for that kind of help. Upon his release from prison, he had one final, fatal bout with cocaine use accidentally ingesting a lethal dose of cocaine. By the following evening, his family had to discontinue life support. I often say that the death bed is a very holy place; however, that night it didn't feel very holy. It felt painful and sad and heart wrenching as I saw the pain and sadness and anger and grief.

Several weeks previously I had received a call from him from prison. I had a conversation with him that day that led to a hope that I cling to. He told me that he had met up with some prisoners who had invited him to a Bible Study and, much to my amazement, he had gone. He had not only attended but listened for the first time to what they taught him. He had recognized his need for a Savior and had experienced what God promises in Scripture: "If the Son shall set you free, you are free indeed." He was free and yet he ultimately could not break his chains of addiction. Like Kathy, he was free to make bad choices. Addiction can be that powerful.

Linda's story on the other hand is very different. Hers was a family that seemed able to cope with normal life issues. She was in helping ministries at two different churches, ministries where she reached out to the hurting whether it was to children or adults. She seemed to cope well with life. Hers was not a tale of addiction or incarceration or a broken marriage. She struggled with depression and she, too, experienced a final straw and just could not take being here one more day.

How do we put this all together? Where can we turn in Scripture? In II Chronicles 20, Jehoshaphat, King of Judah, gives us a clue what to do when the obstacles are too huge. He was facing war with the Moabites and the Ammonites. Some men came to him and told him that a vast army was coming against him. Then Jehoshaphat stood up in the assembly of Judah and Jerusalem at the temple of the Lord and said: "O Lord, God of our fathers, are you not the God who is in heaven? You rule over all the kingdoms of the nations. Power and might are in your hand, and no one can withstand you. O our God, will you not judge them? For we have no power to face this vast army that is attacking us. We do not know what to do, but our eyes are upon you." Whether the vast army is depression, cocaine addiction or something else, we have no power to face it. We do not know what to do, but our eyes are upon you. The Spirit of the Lord spoke to Jehoshaphat through Jahaziel, "Listen, all who live in Judah and Jerusalem. This is what the Lord says to you. Do not be afraid or discouraged because of this vast army. For the battle is not yours, but God's." If only we could remember that in the midst of despair.

Psalm 30 is one of abject despair and unmatched joy. "I will exalt you, O Lord, for you lifted me out of the depths and did not let my enemies gloat over me. O Lord my God, I called to you for help and you healed me. O Lord, you brought me up from the grave; you spared me from going down into the pit. Sing to the Lord, you saints of his, praise his holy name. For his anger lasts only a moment, but his favor lasts a lifetime; Weeping may remain for a night, but rejoicing comes in the morning. When I felt secure, I said, I will never be shaken. O Lord, when you favored me, you made my mountain stand firm; but when you hid your face, I was dismayed. To you, O Lord, I called; to the Lord I cried for mercy. What gain is there in my destruction, in my going down into the pit? Will the dust praise you? Will it proclaim your faithfulness? Help, O Lord, and be merciful to me; O Lord, be my help. You turned my wailing into dancing. You removed my sack cloth and clothed me with joy. That my heart may sing to you and not be silent. O Lord my God, I will give you thanks forever."

What can you do as the caregiver? A good place to start might be to give yourself permission to struggle—face it and admit it, not just to yourself, but to someone else as well. Give yourself time to sort through what is really bothering you. What is the root of your struggle? In fact, ask God to help you sort out the root from the branches. If you only deal with branch issues, you may not understand what is really at the root. Find a listener, because you need to tell your story. Telling your story is not a one-time deal, but rather an ongoing need that may change in intensity or content or complexity, but an ongoing need nonetheless.

God is faithful. He has promised never to leave you nor forsake you. Believe that promise. He is a God of hope. You must be convinced of that fact. He loves you with an incredible love. No doubt about it. You will spend eternity with Him. The assurance of that is unwavering. He gives peace, and you look for that in the midst of turmoil and storms. But sometimes you struggle. The struggles do not disappear because you cling to all of these assurances. Hear this above the doubts and sadness and frustration: God understands those struggles. Run to Him and allow Him to give you the rest that only He can give. This is not a quick fix or an instant solution to your pain. Rather, it is a reminder how much He really loves you, how available He is to you, and how He, the God of the universe knows your needs and your hurt before you come running.

If the pain you are experiencing includes a loved one who has committed suicide, recognize that God is as able to help with that journey as He is with any other. He is able. He is enough. He is faithful. He is with you. He is the Comforter. And He promised. "So do not fear, for I am with you; do not be dismayed, for I am your God. I will strengthen you and help you; I will uphold you with my righteous right hand." Isaiah 41:10. God not only promises to help through fear and dismay, but in the process, He promises to give strength.

Chapter 7

WHAT DO YOU BELIEVE
ABOUT SUFFERING?

"It's obviously not God's will that I kill myself"

CAN WRITE. I JUST DON'T WANT TO HEAR THE
MINDLESS GARBAGE THAT COMES ACROSS AND I CAN'T
WATCH THE CHURCH CHANNELS BECAUSE I KNOW THEY'LL
JUST MAKE ME FEEL LIKE I'VE CHOSEN THE WRONG
THING. IT'S OBVIOUSLY NOT GOD'S WILL THAT I KILL
MYSELF AND IT REALLY BOTHERS ME THAT THE LAST
THING I'LL EVER DO WILL GO AGAINST HIS WILL. IT'S
NOT WHAT I WANT, I SIMPLY FEEL THAT THERE'S
NO OTHER CHOICE ANYMORE. WHEN I COMPARE WHAT
I THINK HEAVEN MUST BE LIKE TO THIS EXISTENCE
(I CAN'T EVEN CALL IT A LIFE ANYMORE) I WONDER WHY
I HAVEN'T ALREADY BEEN ON MY WAY THERE. I TOOK
MY ONLY PICTURE OF GRANDMA AND ONE OF LORENE DOWN
OFF THE FRIDGE TO REMIND ME OF WHO I'M GOING TO
SEE. HOW GLORIOUS TO BE WITH THEM AGAIN IN A PLACE
OF UTTER PEACE. I WISH ENDING IT WERE AS SIMPLE
AS JUST FLIPPING A SWITCH, I WOULD SO DO IT
RIGHT NOW AT THIS MOMENT. I AM READY TO GO,
I JUST WISH IT WASN'T SO HARD TO ACCOMPLISH.
I REALLY REGRET NOT PURCHASING A GUN WHEN
I HAD THE CHANCE. HERE'S HOW HARD IT WILL BE -
FIRST I HAVE TO TIE THE ROPE TO THE BALCONY GUESSING
AT WHAT LENGTH I'LL NEED TO GET IT OVER MY HEAD
ONCE I'M ON THE OTHER SIDE. NEXT I HAVE TO CLIMB
OVER THE TOP OF THE BALCONY AND HOLD ON WITH ONE
HAND WHILE I SOMEHOW GRAB THE NOOSE END AND PUT
IT AROUND MY NECK. THEN I HAVE TO GET IT AS
TIGHT AS I CAN USING ONLY ONE HAND (HAVEN'T

By now, you should get a feel for the incredible pain Kathy was experiencing. As you continue reading pages of her journal, you get a glimpse of her pain and her despair.

It has been said, "Hurt people hurt people". That is the Human Condition." I was reminded how selfish and self-focused we as human beings can become. Some try to convince others that they do not need to worry about the pain they might have caused others to feel because, after all, that's just what people do, they hurt one another.

Hopefully, you react strongly to that statement. The Biblical model of being a Christ follower involves living in relationship with one another, not being the cause of another's pain. As you think about living in relationship, particularly with one who is hurting, what does that look like? If you have a broken arm, that injury is obvious to all you meet, in the grocery store, in your office, at church. But, if you have a broken heart, the pain is hidden. And yet the pain from a broken heart may far surpass the pain of a broken bone. The surgeon who sets your bone is an expert, and you need his expertise in order to make sure the healing process is uncomplicated and complete. It is an amazing gift of God's grace that the kind of expertise needed for the broken heart comes from those God has placed in our lives whose skill set includes love, availability, listening and just simply being a fellow journeyer willing to travel with us.

Part of God's redemption of the pain in our own life is the privilege He gives us to journey alongside another in their pain and suffering. That means as a fellow journeyer we are responsible to-not responsible for. It does NOT mean that we jump into the quicksand with them and become responsible for their situation, for their life, for their crisis. God allows us to be the Shepherd's assistant. He is the One who makes the sheep lie down in green pastures; He leads beside still waters; He is the restorer of one's soul.

What does it look like to walk alongside and help in the restoration process? Think with me about a very old book that needs to be restored. Picture it in your mind's eye. The binding may be torn; the cover may have begun to separate from the pages. In addressing the need, the one who restores books uses the appropriate materials, the proper lighting and a gentle touch to restore the book to the place where it can be salvaged, used, read and kept for generations to come. If we carry our analogy forward to the life of the one who needs to be restored, we must recognize the damage that has been done to the life. We are reminded and instructed to carry each other's burdens; to shine Jesus' light on the wounded, recognizing that the wounded need help. The burden cannot be lifted alone and is at least a two-man job. To understand the burden, we must be willing to take time to listen to their story. However, since grief takes as long as it takes, being available to listen as often as is needed, can become onerous. We need to gather appropriate materials: Does that person need a support network to be drawn around him or her? Need prayer support? Need a small group? We need to be able to bring the "proper lighting" into their life, to help them focus on Jesus, the Light of the World—the Author and Perfecter of our faith.

You may not be the perfect one to help, in fact, you probably won't be, but God will be at work within you, seeking to do His will. Be available; be open; be teachable; just be—and let God do.

Listen to these words of promise from some of my favorite verses in all of Scripture: "Because of the Lord's great love we are not consumed, for his compassions never fail. *They are new every morning*; great is your faithfulness. I say to myself, The Lord is my portion; therefore I will wait for him." Lamentations 3:22-23. That God is a God of new beginnings, is an absolutely true statement. If we were just to dwell on the new beginnings, however, we would misunderstand how we get there from here. New beginnings are especially significant when we have experienced brokenness.

I was in my car one morning, taking some time away from the office. The sky was dark, leaves were blowing off the trees, and the rain came. My heart was heavy with so much pain, so many people suffering. I was driving a bit aimlessly, realizing that my chosen destination would not work. I had planned to wander around the beautiful Hudson Gardens to get a fresh perspective. When I got there, it was raining and cold and windy. No way could I sit on a bench in a beautiful garden-setting to do my journaling. In my aimless wandering, I found myself driving west, thinking and pondering and praying, so much pain and suffering and sadness. And right in the middle of it all I just happened to look up, and I SAW IT. A beautiful rainbow—God's promise. It was amazing. God is definitely a God of hope, a God who keeps His promises. God was giving to me a simple reminder that the rainbow of promise comes out of the darkness in our lives. Had I been sitting in a sun-drenched garden I would still have been feeling heavy and sad and weighted down with the suffering all around. BUT because God had something different, something better for me, I was in my car, headed west with my lights and windshield wipers on, and I experienced the touch of God that a loving Father brings to His children. His rainbow of promise. God is a God of life and of death. If I only see darkness, I miss His faithful promises. If I fail to see the rainbows, I miss His new beginnings.

Chapter 8
TOUGHING IT OUT

"I can only hope it will happen according to the plan. I feel bad that someone will find me-what a terrible thing to do to someone."

8

FIGURED THAT ONE OUT YET). LAST IS THE HARDEST
PART - LETTING GO AND LETTING MYSELF FALL BACK
ABOUT 2 FEET AND DOWN UNTIL THE ROPE CATCHES
AND HOPEFULLY TIGHTENS. THEN IT'S HOW LONG WILL
IT TAKE ME TO ACTUALLY DEE. I'M SOMEWHAT
AFRAID THAT THE ROPE WON'T TIGHTEN ENOUGH TO DO
THE JOB AND THAT I'LL WIND UP DANGLING BY MY
NECK FOR A FEW HOURS UNTIL SOMEONE COMES OUT
AND FINDS ME. I CAN ONLY HOPE IT WILL HAPPEN
ACCORDING TO THE PLAN. I FEEL BAD THAT SOMEONE
WILL FIND ME, WHAT A TERRIBLE THING TO DO TO
SOMONE - WHAT A HORRIBLE SIGHT FIRST THING IN
THE MORNING OR ANYTIME FOR THAT MATTER. BUT IT'S
THE ONLY GOOD WAY I CAN COME UP WITH. IF I
CUT MY WRISTS THERE WOULD BE A HUGE MESS AND
I COULD BE DEAD IN HERE FOR SEVERAL DAYS
WITHOUT ANYBODY KNOWING. THIS WAY I HAVE A
NOTE TAPED TO ME TO CALL UNCLE WALT SO IT WILL
ALL BE TAKEN CARE OF. TOO BAD I DON'T HAVE A
GAS OVEN! I DON'T THINK ANYONE WILL UNDERSTAND
WHY I HAVE TO DO THIS - THEY WILL SAY, "WHY DIDN'T
SHE CHOOSE LIFE?" WHAT NOBODY GETS IS THAT I DON'T
HAVE A LIFE ANYMORE. THE DAYS SEEM ENDLESS, EACH ONE
WORSE THAN THE ONE BEFORE I CAN'T HARDLY GET BREATH
THROUGH MY NOSE BUT I WON'T PUT ON A STUPID FACEMASK
AND BREATHE THROUGH MY MOUTH. I'M EMBARASSED THAT
MY APARTMENT IS SO DIRTY BUT I'M NOT WELL ENOUGH
TO CLEAN AND TOO PROUD TO ASK FOR SOMEONE ELSE TO,

As you think of new beginnings, perhaps in the midst of personal pain and suffering, it is important to understand one's own theology of suffering.

What is your own personal theology of suffering? We are surrounded by broken, hurting people. In fact, if we look in the mirror, we can see the reflection of one who has broken pieces. If we are not careful, we take on a spirit of hopelessness. But that message of hopelessness is not the message of the Gospel of Jesus Christ. God is a God of hope, hope for this broken world, hope for broken people, a message of hope and help for those who hurt.

So your theology of suffering might be Biblically sound or not, because Christian theology is simply an attempt to understand God as He is revealed in the Bible and in God's creation. Perhaps you have never thought of it, and maybe you would disagree that you have your own theology of suffering, but let me ask you a question. When you or someone you love suffers through some kind of loss, what is your reaction? Do you struggle with "Why, God? Why me? I trust you. I believe in you. I don't understand how this could happen." Your theology of suffering may look something like this: "If I pray hard enough, trust hard enough, God will answer and give me the results that I am asking for." If so, it's time to take another look.

Let me give you some ideas of another person's theology of suffering to get us started. The Biblical character, Job, had a theology of suffering which went something like this: "Shall we accept good from God and not trouble?" In all this, Job did not sin in what he said. "But he knows the way that I take; when he has tested me, I will come forth as gold. I know that you can do all things; no plan of yours can be thwarted. Surely I spoke of things I did not understand, things too wonderful for me to know. My ears had heard of you but now my eyes have seen you. I know that my Redeemer lives, and that in the end He will stand upon the earth." Job 23:10 & Job 19:25.

Job's wife however, had a different theology of suffering: "Are you still holding on to your integrity? Curse God and die." Job 2:9.

Abraham when he was tested to lay down his only son, Isaac as a sacrifice on the altar, said: "God himself will provide the lamb for the burnt offering, my son." Genesis 22:8.

Joseph when he revealed himself to his brothers, "I am your brother, Joseph, the one you sold into Egypt. And now, do not be distressed and do not be angry with yourselves for selling me here, because it was to save lives that God sent me ahead of you. For two years now there has been famine in the land, and for the next five years there will not be plowing and reaping. But God sent me ahead of you to preserve for you a remnant on earth and to save your lives by a great deliverance. So then, it was not you who sent me here, but God…You meant it for evil, but God meant it for good." Genesis 50:19-20.

Mordecai (Esther's cousin) "Do not think that because you are in the king's house you alone of all the Jews will escape. For if you remain silent at this time, relief and deliverance for the Jews will arise from another place, but you and your father's family will perish. And who knows but that you have come to royal position for such a time as this?" Esther 4:12-14.

Esther "Go, gather together all the Jews who are in Susa, and fast for me. Do not eat or drink for three days, night or day. I and my maids will fast as you do. When this is done, I will go to the king, even though it is against the law. And if I perish, I perish." Esther 4:16.

I was pregnant with our third child. My husband looked into my eyes one morning and said, "Your eyes are yellow—I wonder what that's all about." I hadn't been feeling well and was experiencing abdominal pain. My doctor also looked into those yellow eyes and had my husband rush me to the hospital, where I was diagnosed with Hepatitis. I remember an overwhelming peace as I lay in that hospital bed, even though we did not at the time know what impact this illness would have on our unborn baby. The next few months were hectic for my husband since I could not even lift the laundry into the washing machine, wash a dish, or prepare a meal. His job more than doubled as he delivered our other two little ones to friends who would watch them for the day, then went on to his teaching job, picked Kirk and Gene up from the friend's home, came home to prepare dinner, do laundry, put the boys to bed in order to get up and do it all over again the next day.

Our baby girl, Kim, was born healthy and strong, in spite of the fact that I had Hepatitis during my pregnancy with her.

We were blessed and grateful. That doesn't mean there are not struggles in life, and pain and suffering. There are parents whose stories are quite different. Many struggle with infertility, or have babies born with disabilities, and who do not have the happy ending we all dream of.

Chapter 9
CHOICES

"It's a good thing I'm leaving because
I'm almost out of clean clothes."

9

ALTHOUGH I HAVE NO IDEA WHO THAT SOMEONE
WOULD BE. I KNOW UNCLE WALT AND AUNT ANNE ARE
GOING TO THINK I'M A COMPLETE SLOB, BUT I DIDN'T
USED TO BE, I ALWAYS KEPT A CLEAN HOUSE, BUT
I'VE BEEN SICK FOR SUCH A LONG TIME AND IT ALL
PILES UP AND GETS A TON OF DUST ON IT. IT DOESN'T
MATTER NOW, BUT IT'S A GOOD THING I'M LEAVING
BECAUSE I'M ALMOST OUT OF CLEAN CLOTHES AND I'M
NOT SURE IF I COULD ACCOMPLISH DOING THE LAUNDRY
TODAY. I SHOULD HAVE GOTTEN MYSELF INTO A
NURSING HOME MONTHS AGO, IT'S RIDICULOUS TO
HAVE AN APARTMENT THAT YOU CAN'T KEEP UP. HELL,
I'M LUCKY IF I CAN ACCOMPLISH A SHOWER. GOING
OFF THAT BALCONY WILL BE VERY DIFFICULT INDEED.
I TAKE IT BACK, THE HARDEST PART ISN'T LETTING GO,
IT'S GOING TO BE JUST GETTING OUT THE DOOR WITH
THE ROPE IN MY HAND. IT MAY SEEM MORBID TO
TALK SO OPENLY ABOUT KILLING MYSELF, BUT IT'S
HELPING ME TO WRITE IT OUT. MAYBE IT WILL
STRENGTHEN MY RESOLVE, I WISH I COULD PRAY
ABOUT THIS BUT IT WOULD BE WRONG TO ASK FOR
GOD'S HELP TO DO SOMETHING HE DOESN'T WANT ME
TO DO ANYWAY. BUT IF GOD WANTS ME TO LIVE
THEN WHY HAS MY LIFE BEEN REDUCED TO NOTHING
BUT MISERY AND TORMENT? HE SEES WHAT I'M GOING
THROUGH, WHY DOES HE WANT ME TO CONTINUE GOING
THROUGH THE MOTIONS WITHOUT REALLY HAVING A
LIFE LEFT TO LIVE? AT THE VERY LEAST I HOPE HE

Suffering Isn't for Sissies

In our western American culture, we tend to do one of 3 things when we are faced with suffering (our own or someone else's):

- We run from it.
- We try to solve it.
- If we can't solve it, we at least want to make it better.

I remember morning after morning on the cross trainer at the gym after our grandson, Jake had been diagnosed with autism, asking God to take the wires in his little brain and make them cross over, to make him better. It took a long time to come to grips with the fact that God has plans for Jake's life that are different and far better than my plans. Jeremiah 29:11 is a very familiar passage of Scripture, "I know the plans I have for you, says the Lord, plans for good and not for evil; to give you a future and a hope."

Suffering is part of the Kingdom story; it is part of the life cycle and it is part of God's story.

Some would choose to declare that life equals loss. I, however, choose to proclaim that life equals hope. Don't ever forget that we have an enemy of our very souls who will attack and accuse and attempt to take us down the "what if" road to a hopeless dead end. God has promised never to leave us nor forsake us, even in the midst of loss. In fact, it's especially in the midst of our losses that we need Him, we need to know that He is there, but perhaps it is at those times that we do not sense Him or feel Him. Those are our "dark night of the soul experiences." We must believe in Paul's teaching from Romans 8, "All things work together for good to those who are called." However, this is a statement that must no longer be regarded as a Biblical mantra for us to utter when we want to deaden pain. For

St. John of the Cross these words were not a cliché but a living and life-sustaining truth.

There are many kinds of losses that can shake one's world. Three years after my Dad's death, my husband was working for a company owned by a friend. That business owner made some unwise investment decisions and my husband lost his job and our retirement account. There were certainly times that followed in which we struggled. In hindsight I recognize that it is okay to struggle. God is our High Priest who understands ALL of those struggles.

There have, of course, been times when I have grappled strongly with life losses and have reacted in very different ways. Through the loss of finances and job, my husband and I learned to trust God in new and creative ways. We were reminded of a time many years before, just a few years out of college, when we lived on very little with three very small children. We needed a certain amount of money and literally watched God provide the exact dollar amount we needed in totally unexpected and unplanned-for ways.

Other personal experiences in our own immediate family shook my world. One in particular, was life-shaking like no other event. My husband went through the cancer that so many men must face, prostate cancer and that in itself was very difficult. The next year I was diagnosed with breast cancer. After previously having had thyroid cancer, the breast cancer was another difficult blow. Then two years later, our two-year-old grandson was diagnosed with Leukemia. That was the most difficult in many ways. I received the word while I was taking a brief study-leave break in the mountains. I raced back to Denver to meet my husband and our son and daughter-in-law and their two other children at Children's Hospital. Thus began a three year battle, and I do mean a battle. We are so grateful for doctors and medicine, though the medicines used for Leukemia have devastating side effects, particularly upon a little body. I was so blessed and proud of our son and daughter-in-law as I watched them try to keep their lives and their family together during that ongoing battle.

Listen to one of our son's journal entries:

"As many parents do, we read the story of Jesus' birth a number of times during the Christmas season, in an attempt to refocus all of the excitement on The One we celebrate this time of year. Each time we sit and read of the nativity, we select a different children's Bible or story book to aid in the telling, and keep it fresh. On this particular morning, I chose to simply forgo all of the beautiful pictorials and use my NIV Bible and paraphrase in a theatrical way as we went along. Now any clear thinking adult would realize that issues dealing with eternity and death, and other themes demanding a certain amount of maturity to grapple with, are best avoided until a certain age. Unfortunately, this adult mentioned, fairly early in the story, offhandedly, in fact almost parenthetically, that God sent Jesus as a baby to save us from our sins, so that when we die we can go to live with Him forever. And this is how our Norman Rockwell moment fell apart:

Mitchell:	*"I don't want to die."*
Dad:	*"Well, no, you won't die for a long time, but when you do…"*
Mitchell:	(Cutting Dad off) *"But I don't want to die."*
Jake:	*"I don't want to die either."*
Mom:	(With a sideways have-you-lost-your-ability-to-reason look at Dad): *"Nobody's going to die."*
Jeremiah:	*"Jesus will make sure I don't die."*
Dad:	*"Uhhh, who wants pancakes?"*
Everyone:	*"YEA…""*

It is throughout difficult journeying times as families or individuals that we come to grips with our need for one another. During this time our family came together, recognizing the need for one another. We are all part of the whole, living in relationship with one another and in need of a God who understands and who cares.

Yet another of Gene's journal entries:

"Jeremiah became sick the last week of March, 2005, with a low grade fever that came and went every few days. The symptoms he experienced over the next four weeks were typical cold symptoms, sluggishness, swollen lymph gland and symptoms not so typical: swollen eyelids, sore legs, and a couple of small bruises with little red pin head sized dots on them. The first visit to the doctor brought nothing more than a suggestion of antibiotics, which we thankfully declined. Thankfully, in hindsight, because antibiotics would likely have falsely elevated his white blood cell count and postponed the red flag which soon thereafter led to his diagnosis.

A worsening of the aforementioned symptoms brought us back to the clinic. Fortunately, the doctor we saw was experienced enough to register alarm at Jeremiah's state. We were thinking perhaps he had been bitten by a spider. Within twenty four hours, this very dear doctor had broken the news to us as gently as possible that our littlest angel had Leukemia. On the same day, she and another guardian angel in a doctor's coat had taken us by the hand, and shaken us gently out of our shock. They had arranged for us to be admitted, sans red-tape the same day to The Children's Hospital here in Denver. Later that day we had the official diagnosis: High Risk Acute Lymphoblastic Leukemia.

Hearing the diagnosis of a catastrophic illness is terrifying. So is being a self-employed former musical star turned voice teacher who is unable to afford health insurance in the United States of America, and hearing that it's one of your children who has that catastrophic illness. From that day, April 14th, 2005, until this, our lives have been transformed. We have become experts on Leukemia, cancer treatments, care of a cancer patient, and learned to negotiate the ins and outs of surviving as an emotionally healthy family, constantly in crisis mode. We have also learned more than ever before about God's grace. Through the kindness and resourcefulness of many family and friends we have found that there is help in our system for families. Today Jeremiah is a healthy boy, wise beyond his years. We are grateful for God's plan."

Chapter 10
DO YOU DESPAIR?

*"I feel like a condemned criminal
knowing exactly when I have to die."*

10

UNDERSTANDS WHY I FEEL LIKE I HAVE NO CHOICE.
IT'S ONLY 1:15 P.M. THAT LEAVES ME 14 HOURS - I FEEL
LIKE A CONDEMNED CRIMINAL KNOWING EXACTLY WHEN I
HAVE TO DIE. I'D LIKE TO TALK TO SOME PEOPLE, LIKE
MY BROTHER BUT WHAT WOULD I SAY? "HEY, HELLO, WELL
I'M GOING TO KILL MYSELF SO I CALLED TO SAY GOODBYE
NOT! I'D PROBABLY BETTER NOT TALK TO ANYONE, NO
MATTER HOW I WOULD TRY TO DISGUISE IT, THE DEPRESSION
AND HOPELESSNESS WOULD SHOW THROUGH. I DON'T THINK
I'VE EVER FELT SO UTTERLY ALONE AND IN THE DARK.
GOING TO HEAVEN MEANS THAT THE DARKNESS WILL ALL
AT ONCE BE SWEPT AWAY AND REPLACED WITH BRIGHT,
WARM RADIANCE AND BRILLIANCE. I JUST CAN'T
IMAGINE HOW GOOD IT WILL FEEL TO LEAVE THIS AWFUL
PLACE BEHIND. I WONDER IF WE SEE THE PEOPLE WE LOVE
RIGHT AWAY OR IF WE HAVE TO GO THROUGH SOME KIND
OF LIFE REVIEW FIRST, DOESN'T MATTER, I'LL BE THERE
AND NOT HERE. I WAS THINKING THIS MORNING HOW I
REGRET NOT BEING CLOSER TO SCOTT'S KIDS, BUT NOW I
THINK IT'S BETTER THAT MY LEAVING WON'T HURT THEM SO
MUCH. I'M RUNNING OUT OF THINGS TO SAY BUT I
DON'T WANT TO STOP WRITING BECAUSE I HAVE NOTHING
ELSE TO DO. THIS IS HOW I IMAGINE DYING - AFTER THE
PAIN AND FEAR RESIDE, AT THE MOMENT OF DEATH
EVERYTHING GOES DARK. THEN ALMOST IMMEDIATELY, LIKE
SOMEONE OPENED A HUGE DOOR IT IS FLOODED WITH THE
MOST BRILLIANT LIGHT, AND OUT OF THE LIGHT COME
WALKING THE PEOPLE THAT WE KNOW WHO LOVE US.

When my Mother was going through her valley of the shadow of death, there were many difficult days and hours. Because my Dad would not admit that she was dying (until the day she actually died), we did not have the freedom to talk openly with Mother about dying, about her fears, about her loneliness. Due to that lack of dialogue, I believe she died a very lonely death, though we surrounded her bed for days and weeks prior to her passing. Dad would call me at work time after time, and I would race to the hospital. Though he would call and wanted us all at her side, he was unable to face the prospect of her death. I remember a particularly poignant visit from two neighbors of my Mom's. They had been neighbors for many years, and they were totally unprepared to be any comfort to my Mom. They sat on the other side of the room, didn't give her a hug or touch of any kind, stayed a very short time, and left, not to return for a second visit. I know how hurtful that visit must have been for my Mom. And yet again, we didn't talk about her feelings, her sadness, her fears, her anger, or any of the emotions she was most likely feeling. My sister, brother, and I shared the bedside vigil. I remember one particularly difficult night. We felt the end was very close, and Mother had been audibly gasping for breath throughout the long night. Then morning came, and Mother woke up and asked what time it was. We couldn't believe that she was still alive; perhaps she was going to get better. That was not to be, of course, but the roller coaster of emotions took its toll on all of us.

In fact, I had a therapist friend tell me during the process of my Dad's death several years later that the roller coaster of dying is one often ridden by family members. The year before my Dad's death, it appeared that he would not be alive at the time of our 25th wedding anniversary. As a surprise for me, my husband had planned a very big celebration with 300+ people, renewing our vows, with our original wedding party and extending that wedding party to include our own children. It was to include a replica of the wedding cake, bridesmaid dresses, and the whole nine yards. It was the beginning of the week before the surprise ceremony, and my Dad asked my husband about the event and indicated that he was looking forward to it. My husband asked him if he thought he'd be able to be there with us, and when my Dad indicated there was no way he was going to miss it, my husband measured him for a tuxedo, and my brother pushed him down the aisle preceding me in a wheelchair. What a treasured memory that is and all the while, the rest of us took yet another roller coaster ride (he died five months later), all doing our own grief work. Often grief work is like peeling back layers of an onion, revealing yet more work to be done.

There is a set of dolls that I keep high in my closet. They're called Russian stacking dolls. From the outside, you see one rather large doll. However, if you look more closely you discover that just at the mid-section there is a line which indicates upon further examination that the top comes off and inside you find another doll. Each consecutive doll is smaller and comes apart and inside is one that is even smaller. The example of the Russian stacking dolls reminds me that inside each of us there is yet another layer. I have found an effective prayer to be, "Lord, help me see the root of this issue. What specifically is at the core of what I'm dealing with? What layer is underneath, hidden?" Of course, some things are obvious, if I have suffered through recent grief and loss in my own life, it seems too evident to question what is at the root. However, many times when we deal with multiple losses, the branches and the root become so intertwined it is difficult to sort through core issues. If I spend time dealing with only branch issues, I may have difficulty being effective in my grief work.

In helping others in their own time of grief, sometimes we just don't know what to do or to say. Every day we and those around us experience loss, change, and transition which we must grieve. Grief is intense emotional suffering caused by loss, and while it is normal, it involves hard work. Does it surprise you that grief not only equals loss but also involves hard work, grief work?

Grief often begins with shock, whether it involves loss of life, loss of relationship, loss of livelihood, loss of the person's living situation, or loss of health. There may be emotional or physical symptoms as well. Some people openly express their grief; others show no emotion. Perhaps you are right in the midst of your own grief work, or you may be helping others work through their loss.

Christians often have the misconceived idea that it is inappropriate to express intense emotions of pain and anger during such a time. Expressing one's grief does not indicate a lack of faith in God; instead it can lead to a deeper understanding of the need for God. Grief is the proper expression of feelings associated with the loss of someone or something significant in our lives, and those who have lost someone close need time to rest and a person with whom they can express their grief.

Many people feel uncomfortable with another's pain and don't know what to say to those who are grieving. Walking beside one who is grieving does not mean that you have the perfect things to say or do. It does mean that you are willing to walk alongside during the process, listening, holding their hand, praying. The more comfortable you are with grief as a natural process, the better able you will be to accept yourself or others who are grieving right where they are and effectively minister to them. And if you are the griever, it means that you will be able to accept the listening friend who wishes to come alongside of you.

Crying, shock and numbness, nightmares, anger, guilt, irritability, restlessness, sleeplessness and loss of appetite all may be symptoms of the normal process of grief. As we walk beside others who go through the valley of the shadow of death, God promises in Psalm 32 that "He will instruct you and teach you in the way you should go; He will counsel you and watch over you." You do NOT have to figure this all out on your own. God will be your teacher. Ask for His help, and He most lovingly and most graciously will give it.

Following my own cancer, I regularly battled the fear of yet another cancer somewhere in my body. Not only is there a lot of cancer in my family, I have experienced caring for many who struggled through cancer treatments and some who ultimately lost the battle and died of this difficult disease. A spirit of fear can be a plague to one who is in the ministry of pastoral care. Understanding the part of Psalm 23 that addresses fear is helpful and comforting. "Yea though I walk through the valley of the shadow of death, I will fear no evil." Though we struggle and are even afraid, we need not fear evil, and we may receive incredible comfort from the phrase which follows: "for Thou art with me…" He has promised never to leave us nor forsake us. He will not fail us; He understands all of our infirmities as we learn in Hebrews 4, and He cares; He truly loves us. Remember, we are all in this life together and God allows us to experience the fellowship of suffering. It just takes a willingness to be vulnerable, expressing your need and asking for help.

Chapter 11
THE HOPE OF HEAVEN

"They Surround Us and Welcome Us Home"

11

THEY SURROUND US AND WELCOME US HOME. THERE ISN'T A
SINGLE BAD FEELING, ALL NEGATIVITY HAS BEEN REPLACED
BY JOY AND AN INCREDIBLE PEACE. THEN PERHAPS
WE ENTER A ROOM WITH A LONG HALLWAY AND ALL
ALONG THE HALL ARE ANGELS IN THEIR SPLENDOR, AND
YOU CAN HEAR THE MOST BEAUTIFUL AND PERFECT
MUSIC. THEN THE ANGELS ALL START TO PRAISE
GOD AND SOMEONE SAYS "BEHOLD THE LAMB" THERE
AT THE END IS A THRONE ON WHICH SITS JESUS AND HE
BECKONS ME TO COME CLOSER. AS I GET CLOSER I CAN
SEE HIS GLORY AND IT IS SO OVERWHELMING THAT I FALL
DOWN ON MY FACE IN WORSHIP OF HIS AWSOMENESS. THEN
JESUS ASKS ME TO RISE AND COME TO HIM SO I DO.
THEN HE OFFERS ME A LOOK AT MY LIFE AND TO MY
SURPRISE IT WASN'T JUST ALL MISTAKES, THERE WAS
SOME REAL WORTH TO IT. AT THIS POINT IF THERE
WERE SADNESS, WHICH THERE'S NOT BECAUSE IT DOESN'T
EXIST ANYMORE THERE, I MIGHT BE SAD THAT I TOOK
MY LIFE ONCE IT'S REVEALED TO ME WHAT I COULDN'T
ACCOMPLISH BECAUSE I LEFT TOO SOON. THAT WOULD BE
THE ONLY REGRET, UNLESS THERE ARE OTHERS IN STORE,
THEN I THINK JESUS ASSIGNS US OUR FUNCTION IN
HEAVEN AS I THINK EVERYONE WILL HAVE A JOB TO DO
FOR ETERNITY. I DON'T THINK WE ALL JUST SIT AROUND
BEING HAPPY. I THINK OUR FUNCTION MIGHT MERROR
OUR LIVES HERE, LIKE WHAT WE'RE GOOD AT. FOR
INSTANCE, GRANDMA MIGHT BE TAKING CARE OF
HEAVEN'S LITTLE CHILDREN OR TENDING TO THE FLOWERS

Kathy's wonderings about Heaven from her journal:

> *"Perhaps we enter a room with a long hallway and all along the hall are angels in their splendor, and you can hear the most beautiful and perfect music. Then the angels all start to praise God and someone says, "Behold the Lamb." There at the end is a throne on which sits Jesus and He beckons me to come closer."*

Our hope is in Him. Jesus said, "In this world you will have suffering." God redeems our own times of suffering by allowing us to come alongside others in their suffering. This, of course, is based upon the assumption that others are honest about their struggles.

I wrote the book, "Helping Those Who Hurt" to help both the wounded and the caregiver to better understand how to help those who suffer.

We can be lulled into a false impression that everyone in our close friend circle is being honest about their struggles. Years ago, Ken and I were in a group of people in which the husband in the family decided he did not want to be married anymore. To all of us in the group, this was a sudden decision, one we did NOT see coming. We were heartbroken, of course, though not nearly as heartbroken as the young wife and child. We all thought we knew the family, that we knew their lives and kept up with one another. Can pain and suffering be hidden in a group? Of course, it can. Sometimes we do not let others into our own lives, and yet we expect that they will let us into theirs. God never intended that we suffer in silence or that somehow to share your struggles means that you are less of a Christ-follower. How can you help carry someone's burdens that you don't even know exist or need carrying?

There are at least two needs we all have: to be taken seriously and to be understood. Thus, as those coming alongside others who are suffering, it is necessary to take their life crisis seriously and to understand. We must never minimize their suffering no matter where we think their pain is on our arbitrary scale. To understand those who suffer, their pain and their need, we must listen. All who suffer loss need to tell their story.

What if there is no one to listen to that story that needs telling? Since that is a basic need they have, you have the privilege of giving them the amazing gift of listening. Nothing replaces your being there for them. God uses His Word, the presence of His Spirit, but God also uses you, with your unique gifting, experience, training, and friendship. Remember, God will be at work within you. Being there for another involves sacrifice, the sacrifice of time and commitment.

As caregivers, we must know what our caregiving is meant to bring about: a life that is balanced and on solid footing. Picture a triangle. When this triangle is balanced on its flat surface, it is solid; when it is standing on the tip, it is unstable. God is our "triangle-tipper." He desires that we understand where our strength comes from and wants us to lean into Him and allow Him to give us a sense of balance.

To have a life that is balanced, we have to have at least as many restorers as drainers. There are people and things in our lives that restore us and people and things in our lives that drain us. There is no way to get around it, that's just the way of life. Life is messy, and caring for people is messy. We must learn to balance those things and people that restore us against the weight of those people and things that drain us. When we have a preponderance of drainers in our life, we will not come back stronger no matter what we are facing.

God teaches us to live in community, in fact, that is the Biblical model of the Trinity, and living in community involves sharing and living with others who energize us. We minister to those who drain us (and we do it gladly as servants), but we must identify those who restore us and be intentional about making sure there is time for them in our life.

What describes you right now? Balanced? Drained? Do you find yourself in a funk or depression of sorts and not sure why? Let's look at root and branch issues again: sometimes it is difficult to even pin point the root, isn't it? I have found it helpful to ask God to help me distinguish the root from the branches. Unless I deal with root issues, I will become distracted with branch issues and continue to be side-tracked and unable to openly identify what it is that is causing my struggle.

"O Lord, you have searched me and you know me. You know when I sit and when I rise; you perceive my thoughts from afar. You discern my going out and my lying down; you are familiar with all my ways." Psalms 139. He really knows you and He loves you and He understands every struggle. The issues may be small but not insignificant. God knows and He cares. He gives strength to the weary and increases the power of the weak. "Even youths grow tired and weary, and young men stumble and fall; but those who hope in the Lord will renew their strength." Isaiah 40:30-31. He understands all the times and seasons when we need strength, when we need renewing and when we need a loving, kind, strong touch from Him, the One who knows us and created us and loved us enough to send His Son to die for us.

Chapter 12
HEARING GOD'S VOICE

"I think the Lord shows us where we belong,
where we'll actually spend eternity."

12

I DON'T KNOW WHAT MINE WILL BE BUT I'D LIKE TO BE A HEAVENLY MUSICIAN. TO BE ABLE TO PLAY THE MOST BEAUTIFUL MUSIC ANYONE HAS EVER HEARD. THEN I THINK THE LORD SHOWS US WHERE WE BELONG, WHERE WE'LL ACTUALLY SPEND ETERNITY. THEN I IMAGINE BEING FREE FOR AWHILE SO I CAN GO BACK AND VISIT WITH ALL THE PEOPLE I LOVE. THERE WILL BE BOTH SETS OF GRANDPARENTS, GRANDMA OF COURSE, LORENE, AUNT RUTH, MY COUSIN JEFF AND MY UNCLE RAY. THEN I THINK WE GET TO HAVE OUR ANIMALS BACK THAT HAVE DIED. THERE WILL BE 4 DOGS AND AT LEAST ONE CAT. I THINK WE GET TO BE WITH OUR PETS FOREVER TOO.

I JUST CALLED UNCLE WALT ABOUT MOVING THE COUCH OUT OF HERE. HE SAID HE WOULD GET BACK WITH ME EITHER TONIGHT OR TOMORROW. I HOPE IT'S TONIGHT. I'M NOT GOING TO WAIT FOR HIM TO COME MOVE IT BUT I WANTED HIM TO KNOW THAT THERE'S A BIG PROBLEM THAT HAS TO BE TAKEN CARE OF BEFORE THE BUGS MIGRATE TO SOMEWHERE ELSE IN THE APARTMENT. NO MATTER WHAT HAPPENED THE COUCH NEEDS TO GO FIRSTTHING, HE WOULD HAVE TO MOVE IT ANYWAY OR RUN THE RISK OF BEING EXPOSED TO THEM AND POSSIBLY TRANSFERRING THEM TO HIS CAR OR HOME ON HIS CLOTHING. IT FEELS BAD TO LIE WHEN HE ASKED HOW I WAS, BUT WHAT CAN I SAY? "BY THE WAY, YOU'RE GOING TO GET A CALL SOMETIME TOMORROW TO LET YOU

I have had some recent experiences that remind me of the need and the call to listen to God's still small voice, but I have to admit at times it is difficult to distinguish His voice from my own, or from the voices of others around me. Does it make sense to you that sometimes your own voice sounds more spiritual than the voice of God? Or that a Christian friend's voice sometimes is the spiritual sounding one, with God coming in a distant second?

When can we hear God's voice, and when we do, what does it sound like? What does it take to hear Him? Our hearing from God is certainly not just at those times when all is still, when we have had a long, peace-filled prayer time with Him, when things are going well for us and our loved ones, when we are experiencing fulfillment and success and satisfaction. Nor is it necessarily at those times when things around us are falling apart, and in desperation we long for and listen to God's voice. Sometimes, it is just in the mundane. Looking at Psalm 46, we are told to "be still and know that He is God," and this following a Psalm that looks at tumultuous times around us, in times of trouble when our world is shaken and everything around us seems uncertain. Because God knows us, inside and out, and loves us perfectly and unconditionally, then He knows our language and exactly what we need, and just the right thing to say to us.

Listen to these phrases: "The Lord is close to the brokenhearted and saves those who are crushed in spirit". Psalm 34. He does not tell us not to be brokenhearted, nor does He try to rebuke us when we feel crushed in spirit. He gives us yet another opportunity to hear from Him, "Trust in the Lord with all your heart and lean not on your own understanding; in all your ways acknowledge Him, and He will make your paths straight." Proverbs 3:5-6. "We wait in hope for the Lord; He is our help and our shield." Psalm 33.

Learning to really listen is an acquired skill. Often, in fact very often, if we are honest with ourselves, we find that we do not concentrate on the skill of listening to others or to God.

Here are a few questions to test yourself on your listening skills: Do you practice ignoring the distractions around you, putting what you have been doing out of sight and out of mind? Do you encourage others to talk, and really be interested in what they have to say? Do you let the other person finish a sentence before jumping in? Do you try to understand the meaning behind the words? Do you listen even though you can anticipate the next word? Do you give your full attention to the one communicating?

This little quiz can easily be applied in person-to-person relationships. But I submit to you that it is also important to think of our person-to-God relationship, which deserves far more of our attention than we are usually willing to give.

"My sheep hear my voice, and they know me?" John 10. Are you one of His sheep? Do you listen for His voice?

Chapter 13
GRIEF TAKES AS LONG AS IT TAKES

"I'm glad I've had a few days now to think about this seriously. It's given me a chance to pray about my life—to say I'm sorry for some things."

13

Know that Kathryn is dead because she hanged herself." I'm thinking of the dumbest things like I'd better water the plants — what difference will it make in a few hours? I'm glad I've had a few days now to think about this seriously. It's given me a chance to pray about my life — to say I'm sorry for some things, to thank him for other things. What's best is the realization I had yesterday that I don't hold anything against anyone — there isn't anyone I haven't forgiven that I needed to and that's the way it should be. With the exception of committing a sin by actually taking my life, my conscience is very clear. God knows all of my regrets, the things I'm sorry for and I know he has already forgiven me of them. I only hope he can forgive my last act in this world. I think I'm going to heaven, I don't think God would keep me from heaven just because I kill myself. I've been strong up until now, but it would take strength I just don't have to continue this awful existence. I just can't stay, I just can't. 12 1/2 hours now and counting. I hope I have the courage to do this. People don't think you have to be brave to kill yourself or even that the opposite is true, but that's wrong. It's going to take all the nerve I can muster to climb those stairs and let go — I need to be more brave than I have ever been. And I'm

I love early summer, the beauty of flowers, green grass, the brightness of sunshine, longer days, shorter nights, barbeques, picnics, time on the deck. And when I think of all these bright, fun, beautiful images as I try to listen for His voice, I find myself reflecting on the Giver of Life and newness and healing and cleanness, and what it is that keeps us from experiencing all of the above. I then ponder forgiveness and the Forgiver, the picture of perfect forgiveness from the Perfect Forgiver. How often does forgiveness become a stumbling block for us? Either we do not feel forgiven, or we are unwilling to forgive those whom we perceive as having wronged us. So we do not avail ourselves of all this beauty and newness.

As Kathy pondered forgiveness in her own life, so must we in ours. She was forgiven by a God who loved her, and was counting on that forgiveness extending beyond her taking her own life. She just couldn't find the strength to go on with her life.

The absolute truth is that forgiveness is available for us. Jesus forgives us. That is the story of an empty cross and an empty tomb. However, we often are not as quick to forgive ourselves or others. Wrapped up in the subject of forgiveness is our ongoing struggle with shame, guilt, and God's grace. Often we do not understand the declaration, "There is therefore now no condemnation for those who are in Christ Jesus." Romans 8:1. We condemn ourselves or others when God does neither.

There are beautiful word pictures in the Old Testament of forgiveness. Joseph, whom his brothers had sold into slavery, was able to declare to them in a spirit of forgiveness and reconciliation. "And now, do not be distressed and do not be angry with yourselves for selling me here, because it was to save lives that God sent me ahead of you." Genesis 45:5. When Jacob was reunited with his estranged brother Esau, Jacob declared, "For to see your face is like seeing the face of God, now that you have received me favorably." Genesis 33:10.

According to a Merriam-Webster dictionary definition, forgiveness means, "to cease to feel resentment against an offender." Our choices matter, and God gives us opportunity to choose to cease to resent another, a conscious choice. "See to it that no one misses the grace of God and that no bitter root grows up to cause trouble and defile many." Hebrews 12:15. Bitterness defiles many, and the bitterness begins in our own heart.

In other words, forgiveness means to choose willingly to give up one's legitimate rights for repayment, and one's tools of punishment, both now and in the future. People believe lies about forgiveness. "I'll just ignore the hurt and bitterness, and eventually it will go away." "When it doesn't hurt anymore, it'll be easier to forgive." "If I can get even, then I'll feel better." "Maybe then I'll be able to forgive." "They need to admit they were wrong." "I'll forgive when and if they ask for forgiveness." Isn't it amazing that we actually choose to nurse a grudge and remain bound and critical and miserable rather than allow God to help us forgive and be forgiven? But even more amazing is the opportunity we have to ask for forgiveness and then to actually forgive.

Reaping the benefits of forgiveness enables us to fully understand the teaching in II Corinthians 1, where we learn that one of the reasons for our own suffering is to be able to comfort others. It's interesting that it does not say we need to share the same kinds of suffering and loss, but rather, the same kind of comfort. In fact, from *The Message:* "He comes alongside us when we go through hard times, and before you know it, he brings us alongside someone else who is going through hard times so that we can be there for that person just as God was there for us. We have plenty of hard times that come from following the Messiah, but no more so than the good times of his healing comfort—we get a full measure of that, too." II Corinthians 1:3-4.

Think back to a time in your own experience, your own life, when you can identify a specific time of suffering. It may be last year, or more recently. With this time of suffering that you are remembering, if you had to quantify it on a suffering scale, (1-10, 10 being the most difficult thing you've ever experienced; 1 being a time where you were troubled or sad but not hugely impacted), where would your remembered life crisis fall? Does it really matter? In some ways, most definitely. But as far as your need for comfort, no, not really. That same perspective is true in the life of those around you, those lives God may allow you to touch. Whether or not on your own rating scale your suffering seems higher, more difficult, more life-altering, isn't the significant thing in the II Corinthians passage. The important thing for you to remember is the comfort you received. God takes our pain seriously; He understands; in fact, in Hebrews we read that "we do NOT have a high priest who is unable to sympathize" He understands it all, no matter where on the scale your pain falls. He is right there. And He understands the one into whose life you have the privilege of speaking.

When God calls us to come alongside another who is suffering, we need to take that life crisis seriously. If to be heard is a basic need someone has, you have the privilege of giving them that unconditional gift. I remember being called out late at night by a young woman who was new to our church. Her husband had just taken his life. When I arrived at the house, I found a scene of total chaos, which is often the case in a suicide or any sudden death. Friends and neighbors were pouring into the house. There were groups that were talking loudly; others were whispering; still others were just plain obnoxious. This young wife needed someone to listen, quietly listen. I had the privilege of being in that role, of taking her into her own kitchen, apart from the chaos, asking a couple of open-ended questions, and just sitting with her.

God wants us to recognize and share emotions; this is another gift you give. It is important to recognize that it is not enough to share thoughts, but it is important to share feelings as well. Depression, sadness, loneliness, fear, and anger are emotions that can surface and must be shared.

We are to treat others' crises with dignity and respect, no matter the age. If a teen has broken up with a boyfriend or girlfriend, his or her world has been turned upside down. If a businessman has just lost a major account and knows that his job is in jeopardy, his livelihood is in question. If an elderly wife has just been told that her husband has terminal cancer, her future living situation is called into question. Irrespective of age and stage of life, each one needs to be listened to and taken seriously.

In the midst of helping others, we need an outlet for our pain, someone to whom we can tell our own story.

I had been ministering to several families during a given period of time who had lost loved ones, one of them a very dear friend. As the Director of Caring Ministry, most often when a family in our church body has a death, I walk through that death with that family. So I had walked through several deaths, several funerals prior to the time of my dear friend's death. I not only walked through her death, was at the hospital when she died, helped plan and implement the funeral, and support her husband, but I struggled with my own grief. It was very real, and hard, and I needed to be able to process with someone.

How about you? Who is it in your life with whom you share your pain?

Remember, grief takes as long as it takes. We cannot rush the process, the care needed, the story-telling, the movement from one stage of the grieving process to another. Also, remember that we go through the process of grief for many more things than death. Grief and loss issues, as I've mentioned above, surround death but also include many other types of pain from multiple origins. Sometimes we try to rush another through their grief. It's almost like we give them a certain (though ill-defined) timeline in which to grieve. If they aren't "all better," whether it's from a miscarriage, a divorce or broken relationship, a family issue, an employment issue, or some other loss, we become impatient. We forget that grief takes as long as it takes.

We must try to be available when and where needed. Ministry is messy and often inconvenient. To be available for the one going through pain, we must be available when the need arises, not when all of our schedule and ducks are in a row. Nothing replaces the gift of presence, your being there for them. We must not shy away from the tough stuff, whether in our own suffering or that of another. Often there is a pink elephant in the living room that we tend to dance around. We need to identify the problem which sometimes involves un-resolved family issues, and sometimes a lack of forgiveness.

Understand that guilt often accompanies suffering. For unexpected deaths this is often one of the stages that is most difficult to work through; "if only I had"; "if only I had not." Deaths by suicide are particularly difficult because often the parent or the spouse or the friend or the caregiver feels there must have been something they could have done to prevent the death.

In coming alongside, we must not assume. Some problems may surface quickly and be obvious, but the crisis that is evident may just be the tip of the iceberg. Asking questions that are open, "tell me about...", rather than asking "how are you feeling?" helps to give opportunity for the person to express and share. When you are grace-filled and non-judgmental the person in crisis may be more willing to open up about what is really going on.

As the caregiver, we primarily need to recognize that we cannot fix anyone's pain. There are a few helpful things to do—recognize and acknowledge their loss; check in often, being careful to ask if this is a good time to talk, and don't hesitate to use the deceased's name. Remember that everyone grieves in unique ways. This is true no matter what the loss. While it is helpful to understand the stages of death and grief, it is not helpful to try to cram someone into a grief mold, expecting that either they are going to grieve in the same way as someone else, or that they are going to go through these stages in a neat, orderly fashion. Grieving is messy. In the midst of messy, disorderly lives, people run out of hope. They struggle. How do we help in those struggles?

All around us we see news reports of hopelessness. A young man takes his life. We cry out, "Oh, God, what is going on in our world?" There are so many who are hurting and hopeless and full of despair. They see no way forward. Their best way is the way out: out of despair, out of pain, out of trouble, out of hopelessness. But, is that the only alternative? The only answer? The only path? God is a God of hope, hope in the midst of pain; hope in the center of the storm; hope in the hurt.

When suicide is a choice, often people are so disoriented that choice is almost secondary. The suicide involves choice, but can't simply be attributed to a bad decision. To the one ending his or her life it seems the best alternative. It is a permanent solution to what may be a temporary problem. Simple but true.

God has promised never, ever to leave us nor forsake us, not now, not ever. How does the fact that God will not leave our side help? A friend and I sat with a woman today who has just been put in hospice care. She told me that she was scared. When I asked her to tell me more about that, she said she was afraid to be alone. I then said, "what if I could tell you that you do not ever have to be alone again because God has promised never to leave your side. That is hope".

What is the difference between the young man who suffers humiliation and exposure and despair and chooses to end his life and the one who struggles and stays in the pain and turmoil and tension of his struggles? Might the difference be hope, hope in the midst of pain and suffering and despair, hope that no matter how bad it gets there is a future? There is a way through this hard time? There is a personal God who cares and offers help.

We must take all suicide threats seriously even when we suspect that it is a plea for attention. Inquire about the threats, about a possible suicide plan and the means to carry out that plan. Be a good listener. Make an open-ended statement, such as "I am so sorry that you hurt so much." Allow expression of feelings and accept those feelings. The person who is hopeless cannot see his or her way clear to come up with a plan of hope. We can help them with that plan, help them discover their options, put them in touch with resources and even offer to go with them to a counselor or agency that can help.

"May the God of hope fill you with all joy and peace as you trust in him, so that you may overflow with hope by the power of the Holy Spirit." Romans 15:13. The God who made us, understands how to fill us with hope in the midst of any situation.

Chapter 14
THE COMMONALITY OF GRIEVING

*"In order to judge me right or wrong, a person would
have to know what this "life" is doing to me and
there's only one person who knows how that feels."*

14

Doing it not because it's right, because it is absolutely wrong, but because it's the best thing given all the circumstances. In order to judge me right or wrong, a person would have to know what this "life" is doing to me and there's only one person who knows how that feels. I haven't arrived at this decision lightly; it is the last resort - in the absence of hope that anything is going to get any better and given that every day proves worse than the last, it is the option that makes the most sense. I want to be in heaven instead of here anymore. I don't want one more day to go by to find out how much worse and more dark it can get. It ends at 3:30 tomorrow morning and that's just how this all played out. I played, but now it's played out. I need to separate out the Christian CD's for Kevin - I'll just put them in a bag and leave them on the chair. I'm glad I thought of it - Elaine would never listen to them, I don't even know if she'll take the rest, whatever it makes no difference to me. I'm going to go lay down for awhile, I'm really tired because I couldn't sleep last night or this morning. Still couldn't sleep because my arms are itching too badly, I had some dry skin that itched and when I scratched it I got a bunch of these red welts, they look like bug bites but they're just from scratching with my nails. Maybe lack of sleep is a good thing, maybe

I have recently felt assaulted by evil. As I grapple with the incredible horror of a little girl who was kidnapped and dismembered and know the sadness of our grandson who was a classmate of hers, I have not only struggled with my own emotions of sadness and anger and bewilderment, I have had to come face to face with the turmoil of the unthinkable. On the one hand, I know and serve a loving God who is good and just and sovereign and holy. I know He could have stopped the perpetrator from carrying out this senseless, horrible act. I know He could have protected this little ten-year-old girl who was just doing normal kid stuff on her way to meet up with a friend to walk the short distance to school. Yet she never made it, either to meet the friend or to get to school. I know God loved her; I know He loves her family; I know He is good; I know He cares. All of those things I know.

Yet the news is full of pain as are our lives:

- A young female Starbuck's barista kidnapped and murdered and a neighbor arrested, leaving a young husband to weep and mourn and not understand.
- A young father, a kind, loving, godly man, dying of cancer.
- A woman, rejected years earlier by her mother, tired of the struggles of this life on a daily basis, choosing to take matters into her own hands, ending her life. Hers is an ending of incongruities, wanting no more pain in this life and yet assured of the hope of Heaven and being with Jesus and with her Grandma.

I know that I can't explain why or fix the pain or answer the questions. Jesus said, "In this world you will have tribulation, but be of good cheer, I have overcome the world." John 16:33. "God, how can I be of good cheer when faced with something so terrible? How can I answer those who have asked the question, God could have protected her; why didn't He?" In such a time as this, I must deal with the deeper questions of the emotions of pain and suffering, but I also must focus on what I do know. I know that we have an enemy of our souls who tries to rob us of hope and joy and peace. I know that until that time when God makes everything all right, we will struggle and suffer. I know that God is true and a Redeemer and is a Righteous God who one day will take away all pain and suffering and erase the hurt from our hearts and wipe away the tears from our eyes. I know that little 10-year-old girl is in Heaven with Jesus and enjoying a life that we can now only imagine. I know that He promises to walk with us through the valley of suffering. I have confidence that what He promises, He will do; He will never leave us nor forsake us. I know that greater (far greater) is He who is in us than he who is in the world.

If you are in the valley of suffering as you read this and are hurting or angry or confused or pondering, know that all of those emotions are valid. Know that God loves you. Know that He one day will bring justice and peace. Know that He promises peace in the midst of your storm, and He invites you to come to Him now.

Jesus loves you. This I know. Because the Bible says so.

What do the following have in common?

- A man said he broke down in tears when he and his wife stepped into the food pantry near their home in an affluent suburb. The gentleman who is an engineer with a Master's Degree, had lost his job at a technology company a month earlier. "It was hard to take," recalls the 52 year old who says he spotted a longtime friend at the same center and tried to avoid being seen. "I've never had to do anything like that in my life."

- A young woman had just been rejected from being included in a particular group she had sought admittance into. She was hurt, depressed, felt betrayed, and angry (though she didn't admit to the latter). She stopped by my desk and poured out her story. There was a lot of blaming, declaration of innocence on her part, and a sense of disbelief and abandonment.

- A senior citizen is currently a patient in the ICU unit at a local hospital. She is 90 years old; has never been married; has no children; and lives with a dear friend of many years, who is herself 93. She may or may not get better from the emergency surgery. She has never wanted to talk about her own funeral planning and yet this day, she talked a lot about Heaven, dying, going to be with Jesus, and expressed that the funeral service we had for her other friend was beautiful, the best one she had ever gone to.

So, what is the common link? All of these folks are hurting, need to be cared for by someone who is willing to take time to help them in their pain. Too often, when many are put in these situations, they don't know how to help. They don't know what to say. They feel they have to fix the problem. They aren't sure when to keep silent.

We all have those in our lives who are hurting. We tend to make the solution too complicated; there *must* be something we are to do other than listen. And yet one of the most beneficial things you can do for that person in your life is to listen while they tell their story. I'm not saying that you need to fix another's predicament; in fact, often when someone comes to us with a hurt in their lives, they do not want us to fix it. They want us to listen.

Listening is a skill that must be thoughtfully and deliberately pursued and refined. To be quick to listen and slow to speak is indeed a gift. Do you know what it feels like to be really, thoroughly listened to? On the other hand, have you experienced what it's like to be pouring out your heart to a friend, only to realize that they are distracted, not listening, looking around the room, texting on their phone and obviously waiting for you to finish? Pretty disappointing, isn't it?

Think of a time in your life when you needed a friend. Was it an issue with your boss, with your family, with your neighbor? My guess is that you did not expect or even want your friend to fix the issue. Wouldn't it have been great to have a non-judgmental, caring, unbiased listener alongside of you?

Try an experiment during the next week: spend more time listening than talking. Listen with no agenda, no judgment, no need to fix or get your own point across; just listen. You'll be glad you did.

Chapter 15
A TIME FOR ALL THINGS

"I'll be too tired to be afraid when it's time."

15

I'LL BE TOO TIRED TO BE AFRAID WHEN IT'S TIME, NOW 10 HOURS AWAY. WITH ANY LUCK I'LL BE IN HEAVEN BEFORE THE SUN COMES OUT AGAIN. IT IS GOING TO DEPEND ON LUCK. I JUST HAD A SCARY THOUGHT - WHAT IF THE ROPE PULLING TIGHT CAUSES MY NECK TO BREAK? I WONDER IF THAT WOULD HURT MUCH? DON'T THINK ABOUT IT, IF THAT HAPPENS THE ROPE WILL BE TIGHT ENOUGH TO KILL ME IN A FEW MINUTES. I WISH I KNEW HOW LONG IT WOULD TAKE, I DON'T WANT TO BE LINGERING THERE FOR AN HOUR SLOWLY NOT BEING ABLE TO BREATHE, OF COURSE I WANT IT TO BE FAST AND SOMEWHAT PAINLESS. THERE'S JUST NO WAY TO TELL HOW IT WILL BE, THAT'S THE GLARING FLAW IN MY PLAN. IT'S ALMOST 6:30 AND I'M STARTING TO GET NERVOUS, WORRIED THAT I WON'T BE BRAVE ENOUGH. IT'S THE LETTING GO AND FREE-FALLING BACKWARD THAT I'M AFRAID OF. IT WILL TAKE ALL OF MY STRENGTH TO LET GO. I DON'T KNOW WHAT TO DO TO KEEP MY COURAGE UP EXCEPT KEEP TELLING MYSELF THAT IT MUST BE TOMORROW MORNING - THERE'S NO POINT IN WAITING ANYMORE. TODAY FEELS LIKE IT'S BEEN 3 DAYS LONG, TOMORROW WILL ONLY BE WORSE. I LOOK AT THE PHOTOGRAPHS AGAIN TO REMIND ME OF WHAT'S WAITING ON THE OTHER SIDE OF DEATH. EVEN IF IT TAKES AWHILE TO ACTUALLY DIE, IT'S STILL JUST A SHORT TIME WHEN COMPARED TO ETERNITY, MERELY MINUTES COMPARED TO FOREVER. IT JUST STRUCK ME HOW YOUNG I AM, IF I WERE IN GOOD HEALTH I COULD EXPECT TO LIVE ANOTHER 40 YEARS, THAT'S A WHOLE OTHER LIFETIME. YES I AM TOO YOUNG TO DIE, BUT I'M NOT IN GOOD HEALTH AND

As you are beside the bed of the dying, how do you come to grips with your own mortality and theirs as well? There isn't a magic formula for bedside care to the dying; however, there are things that can be more helpful than others. Silence is precious; guard your words carefully. Pay attention to whose needs you are meeting—yours or the dying? Allow the dying person to set the tone and let your demeanor match theirs, while at the same time being loving and pleasant. In other words, there are certain behaviors that can be irritating, such as inappropriate or unwanted humor, and/or incessant talking. While there may be many people in and out of the room, there needs to be one, or at least a very small number, who serves as point person who can advocate for the patient, guarding him or her from conversation that is too loud or too boisterous, too many people around the bed at once. Spending time with the dying can cause you to grapple with your own mortality, so allow yourself to grapple. Be sensitive to the dying person's desire for prayer and Bible reading. Be the one bold enough to gently ask if he or she is afraid.

I had an experience where I asked the dying patient if she was afraid. This was an important question for her to be able to respond to, and yet it was too difficult for family members to pose. She nodded that she was in fact afraid and did indeed want to have me share Scripture with her. It was wonderful to be able to read to her from the Psalms. "Even though I walk through the valley of the shadow of death, I will fear no evil," brings tremendous comfort. The dying person needs to be able to express his or her feelings.

As a caregiver, you need to take time to acknowledge and process your own grief.

Ecclesiastes 3:1-8: "There is a time for everything, and a season for every activity under heaven:

A time to be born and a time to die,

A time to plant and a time to uproot,

A time to kill and a time to heal,

A time to tear down and a time to build,

A time to weep and a time to laugh,

A time to mourn and a time to dance,

A time to scatter stones and a time to gather them,

A time to embrace and a time to refrain,

A time to search and a time to give up,

A time to keep and a time to throw away,

A time to tear and a time to mend,

A time to be silent and a time to speak,

A time to love and a time to hate,

A time for war and a time for peace."

It's important to remember, however, that your season may not be another's season. "He has made everything beautiful in its time." Ecclesiastes 3:11.

What season are you in right now?

A growth season?

A re-grouping season, which often comes after a growth time?

A hurting or suffering season?

A grieving season?

A transition season?

A season of peace?

A season of malaise?

It is very important to identify what season you are in before you can hope to reach out to those around your dinner table or in the office cubicle next to yours. If you don't know where you are, you can't know where to go, either for yourself or in giving directions to another.

Chapter 16
HELPING OTHERS TO HOPE

Nothing is normal. After today I feel like I've been here forever waiting for things to change for the better, but it never comes."

16

NOTHING IS NORMAL. AFTER TODAY I FEEL LIKE I'VE BEEN
HERE FOREVER WAITING FOR THINGS TO CHANGE FOR THE
BETTER, BUT IT NEVER COMES. GRANDMA AND LORENE BOTH
LIVED TO BE 79 AND THEY JUST WANTED TO SEE 80, BOTH
DIED FROM CANCER. IF I HAD CANCER I WOULDN'T BE
ENDING IT BECAUSE I WOULD KNOW THERE WAS AN EVENTUAL
END. BUT I COULD KEEP EXISTING LIKE THIS FOR AWHILE
EXCEPT FOR NOT BEING ABLE TO TAKE CARE OF EVERYTHING.
I'm TIRED OF GOING OVER AND OVER THE SAME THINGS,
I'm JUST WRITING FOR SOMETHING TO DO AND TO KEEP IT
IN THE FRONT OF MY MIND WHAT I MUST DO IN 8 SHORT
HOURS. THERE WILL BE NO EXCUSE FOR NOT ACCOMPLISHING
MY GOAL IN THE MORNING, I SIMPLY MUST NOT FAIL.
I FORGOT, UNCLE WALT CALLED AND SUGGESTED I HIRE
SOMEONE TO HAUL OFF THE COUCH, HE THOUGHT IT HAD TO BE
TAKEN AWAY, I TOLD HIM IT JUST HAS TO GO OUT TO THE
DUMPSTER AND SO HE'S GOING TO TRY TO GET MY UNCLE KEN
TO HELP HIM. WELL, IT WILL BE UP TO THEM NOW AS WELL
AS EVERYTHING ELSE IN THIS PLACE. IT'S TOO BAD YOU
CAN'T JUST CALL GOODWILL AND HAVE THEM COME GET
EVERYTHING, WHICH IS WHERE MOST OF IT SHOULD GO.
BUT THEY DON'T DO THAT ANYMORE, YOU HAVE TO TAKE
THE DONATIONS IN YOURSELF. I DON'T KNOW WHAT
UNCLE WALT IS GOING TO DO WITH ALL THESE THINGS,
MAYBE OUTSIDE OF THE FURNITURE AND THINGS THEY CAN
USE, HE COULD JUST HIRE SOMEONE TO HAUL EVERYTHING
TO THE DUMP OR SOMETHING. I WOULDN'T KNOW WHERE
TO START. I FEEL BAD THAT I DON'T HAVE THE

I love this verse from Elizabeth Barrett Browning:

> *"Earth's crammed with Heaven,*
> *And every common bush afire with God,*
> *But only he who sees takes off his shoes*
> *The rest sit round it and pluck blackberries.*

It reminds me of the phrase in Psalm 51, "Let me hear joy and gladness." The context of that verse is that David is pouring out his very heart to God after Nathan the Prophet has come to him to confront him with the sin, of committing adultery with Bathsheba. As we allow God to help us see joy and gladness around us, transformation happens, our own metamorphosis. We are like the butterfly. The butterfly begins life as an egg, emerges as a caterpillar and undergoes a complete change in body form. The caterpillar looks nothing like the winged butterfly. After hatching from the egg, the caterpillar spends most of its time eating leaves and gaining weight. Isn't that a picture of us as baby followers of Christ? "If anyone is in Christ, he is a new creation." II Corinthians 5:17. Baby creations have to eat and gain weight, and that's what we have to do. The caterpillar undergoes several molts of its skin until it becomes full grown and has accumulated enough body mass to carry it through the entire life cycle, including the adult phase. We, too, have to morph many, many times by shedding molts of our skin and going through a variety of seasons of life.

For all of us, no matter how difficult our life is at the present time, God is "morphing" us, changing us, growing us.

Chapter 17
LISTEN LONG AND HARD; CONTENTMENT

*"Oh well, it doesn't really matter
to me what happens to my remains."*

17

MONEY FOR MY CREMATION, AT LEAST NOT UNTIL I GET PAID ON THE 1ST, BUT ANYWAY, HE'S GOING TO GET THE $20,000 FROM MY INSURANCE SO I GUESS HIS EXPENSES WILL EVEN OUT. STILL, I HOPE THAT NONE OF IT IS A HARDSHIP ON HIM. I DON'T EVEN THINK HE KNOWS THAT I WANT MY ASHES TO BE PUT IN THE SOUTH PLATTE RIVER. OH WELL, IT DOESN'T REALLY MATTER TO ME WHAT HAPPENS TO MY REMAINS. I WONDER IF THE POLICE WILL TAKE MY BODY AWAY FROM HERE AND THEN UNCLE WALT WILL HAVE TO SEND THE CREMATORS TO THE POLICE TO PICK UP MY BODY. I IMAGINE THE POLICE WILL WANT THEIR CORONER TO VERIFY DEATH AND CAUSE OF DEATH. I WONDER IF THEY'LL DO AN AUTOPSY. I MEAN, I'M SURE THE POLICE WILL BE CALLED, THAT'S WHAT I WOULD DO IF I FOUND SOMEONE HANGING. I SUPPOSE THE FIRE DEPARTMENT WILL HAVE TO COME GET ME DOWN, IT WILL TAKE A LADDER. I IMAGINE A LOT OF PEOPLE WILL SEE ME SINCE IT WILL TAKE AWHILE TO GET ME OUT OF HERE, I'M NOT HAPPY ABOUT BEING A SPECTACLE, BUT IT HAS TO BE PUBLIC SO I'LL BE FOUND RIGHT AWAY. IF I DIED IN HERE, NOBODY WOULD KNOW AND I DON'T KNOW HOW LONG IT WOULD TAKE UNCLE WALT TO FIGURE OUT THERE WAS SOMETHING WRONG I COULD BE BADLY DECOMPOSED BY THEN, ESPECIALLY WITH THE HEAT. NO, A PUBLIC SUICIDE IS BETTER ALL THE WAY AROUND. NO ONE CAN SAY THAT I HAVEN'T THOUGHT THIS THROUGH. I'VE BEEN CHAIN SMOKING ALL EVENING, PARTLY BECAUSE I'M NERVOUS AND PARTLY BECAUSE IT DOESN'T REALLY

A subject for consideration when investigating the issue of suicide is that one of life's major struggles involves a lack of contentment. Are you content? If you are like me, your answer might be something like, "sometimes, with certain things, at certain times, most of the time, not right now, I was last month," all over the board. Recently while on a wonderful, beautiful, restful vacation I spent some time looking out upon a lovely setting, pondering contentment. It should have been easy to be content in my setting, but even in that idyllic moment, I found myself struggling.

I realize that Jesus calls us to be content, in fact, here are two phrases from the Bible. "For I have learned the secret of being content in any and every situation." Philippians 4:12. "Be content with what you have because God has said, never, ever will I leave you, never will I forsake you." Hebrews 13:5.

How do I learn the secret of being content? Sometimes in trying to get to the heart of a matter, it helps to discover what it is NOT. The key to contentment is definitely NOT found in having an abundance, "if I have enough, then I'll be content." After all, what is enough? My measuring stick of enough is very likely different from yours, whether in things or in relationships. The secret rather has to do with our focus or preoccupation. Contentment is a necessary learned act of obedience. Learning to be content can help us through many life difficulties whether our struggle is financial or relational, emotional or spiritual. Contentment is a growth journey, one that I cannot do on my own. God has promised to strengthen me, empower me, and help me learn to appreciate what I have.

For some, the challenge of being content involves not having what someone else has and wishing you did, not having the right kind of vacation, the right kind of car, the right kind of house, the money to shop whenever, wherever, the right kind of retirement, better health, the right kind of college for your children. For others, the issue involves relationships. Wishing that you had the kind of relationship with your spouse, your daughter, your mother or your friend that someone else has with their spouse, or daughter or relative or friend. The issues may concern our health or our career, our education, or our mental prowess.

So, when we struggle, when we are discontent, what does it take to grapple and to choose a path of contentment? Some have a more difficult journey than others and take two steps forward and three back. Perhaps all of us have a more difficult time in some areas than others.

In trying to develop a heart that is content, does it sound too simplistic to practice the act of thankfulness? "Lord, I may not have what she has, but thank you for what you have given to me. Because you know me better than I know myself, you know what I need, you know what I have and you really, really love me. That is enough. You are enough."

I'm not there yet but I'm on the journey, learning to be content. Maybe that is enough for now.

As Ecclesiastes says there is a time for everything. A time to suffer and during those times of suffering, the opportunity to experience God's peace. Sometimes our discontent takes on the form of blaming God. As Mary says of her brother, Lazarus' death, "Lord, if you had been here, my brother would not have died." John 11:32. Who or what is your Lazarus right now? Is it someone or something in your family or yourself, a health issue, the loss of a loved one? "Lord, if only you had…I wouldn't be struggling like this."

Chapter 18
CRISIS COMES IN ALL FORMS

"I don't want anyone to have to pay;
I've always taken care of myself."

18

MATTER. I WAS JUST LOOKING AND MY INHALED MEDICATIONS ARE BRAND NEW NOT USED, GUESS I DIDN'T HAVE TO BUY THOSE. I ALSO HAVE ENOUGH SODA FOR A MONTH AND ABOUT 20 CANS OF SOUP I HAVEN'T USED. I GUESS THEY CAN JUST DONATE ALL THE CANNED FOOD, ETC.. MAYBE THEY CAN USE THE CLEANING SUPPLIES. I HAVE 2 FULL BAGS OF TRASH THAT I HAVEN'T BEEN ABLE TO TAKE OUT. THIS PLACE IS DOWNRIGHT DISGUSTING. I HAVE 4 PACKS OF CIGARETTES LEFT, I DON'T KNOW WHY I BOUGHT SO MANY, I HOPE THEY JUST THROW THEM AWAY. I WISH I COULD HAVE QUIT, I DON'T KNOW WHY THAT WAS ALWAYS THE HARDEST THING TO GIVE UP. I'VE HAD THE "QUIT PATCHES" FOR A COUPLE OF MONTHS, I JUST NEVER DISCIPLINED MYSELF. IT'S GOOD THAT I WON'T HAVE TO PAY THE RENT OR COMCAST OR EXCEL. THAT SHOULD LEAVE ENOUGH MONEY FOR MY CREMATION AND OTHER EXPENSES. I THINK THE WAY THEY WORK IT IS THEY OWE YOU THE LAST MONTH SINCE THE PAYMENTS STARTED ONE MONTH OUT. ANYWAY, I ASKED UNCLE WALT NOT TO NOTIFY SOCIAL SECURITY OR LOCKHEED MARTIN UNTIL AFTER THE 3RD. IT'S EITHER THAT OR SOMEONE ELSE HAS TO PAY TO HAVE MY BODY TAKEN CARE OF. I DON'T WANT ANYONE TO HAVE TO PAY FOR ME, I'VE ALWAYS TAKEN CARE OF MYSELF. 7 HOURS TO GO, IT'S GOING BY FAST AND I'M GETTING REALLY NERVOUS. LOOKING AT THE PHOTOGRAPHS AGAIN TO REMIND ME. THE PICTURE OF GRANDMA HAS HER HOLDING ME AT ONE YEAR OLD, I THINK THAT'S WHEN SHE FIRST MET ME. SHE HAS A GREAT BIG SMILE,

Many of us have been touched by the pain of suicide, a pain that at times has tangible, physical components and spreads to all of our being, our body, our emotions, our heart, our spirit. Pain that so engulfs us can leave us gasping for air and grasping for hope. Whatever specific circumstances lead people to suicide, it is almost certain that they were experiencing deep inner turmoil. Where can we go for help in such tragedy? The Bible invites us to go to God both with our concern about the eternal destiny of the one who committed suicide as well as for strength to minister to grieving victims. Remember, "The Lord is close to the brokenhearted and saves those who are crushed in spirit." Psalm 34:18.

The early church took a harsh stand against suicide; however, in more recent times, many denominations have recognized that people who attempt suicide need to be helped rather than punished and survivors need to be helped to grieve, not condemned.

For most survivors, death by suicide embarks one on a journey of very complicated grief. It is possible to lose sight of the fact that all the stages of grief are still there: sadness, anger, depression, bargaining, acceptance, and that one goes back and forth and up and down and in and out through all of the stages. It is, of course, compounded with the "why's" and the "why didn't I's?" and with the shock and the denial of the violence of a death by suicide. Grief in general is difficult to deal with, but when the death results from suicide, additional factors are involved. The shock is more intense and is accompanied by anger, guilt, helplessness, and a long list of unanswered questions. All this swirls around in your mind while you try to hang on, searching for a sign that you will survive this trauma. Obviously, receiving the news and accepting the reality are entirely different. When you hear the tragic news, all you can do is begin to process it. The process takes time. It cannot be rushed. In the past, the model for Christians was to keep a stiff upper lip and to endure the pain and agony of the loss with little or no expression and with the shame that led to suffering in silence. Many Christians now recognize that grief does not express a lack of faith in God, rather it can lead us to a deeper understanding of our need for God.

Anyone caregiving after a suicide should remember to be an encourager and a grace-extender. Though we want to help and we project what we would want in a similar life circumstance, it is important to remember that some people are very private people who choose to grieve privately. Your care for the private person will look different; however, God will give you wisdom how to give care through a phone message, a text, an email, a card, a silent hug.

Even in the best of relationships, disagreements arise. But in actuality, when people are in the midst of struggling through the death of a loved one by suicide, there may be more points with which to take issue. It is at those sticky times that we need to be dispensers of God's grace. What might be a good way to handle some of those disagreeable moments? How may we extend God's grace to the one who is grieving?

I love the following, taken from "A Chaplain's Daily Prayer:"

"Grant that I may listen and hear the true heart-felt needs of those around me. May I not be so wrapped up in myself, and my own issues, that I fail to meet people where they are emotionally and spiritually. Give me the courage to come from my heart and not just my head. May my words be few, and may they be words of truth, empathy, and hope spoken in love. I pray that each person to whom I minister will be brought at least one step closer to you because of my being with them. Lord, may it be so with me."

There should be no condemnation: "Therefore, there is now no condemnation for those who are in Christ Jesus." Romans 8:1 In the Book of Romans in the New Testament we read "Who will bring any charge against those whom God has chosen? It is God who justifies. Who is he that condemns? Christ Jesus, who died—is at the right hand of God and is also interceding for us. Who shall separate us from the love of Christ? Shall trouble or hardship or persecution or famine or nakedness or peril or sword? For I am convinced that neither death nor life, neither angels nor demons, neither the present nor the future, nor any powers, neither height nor depth, nor anything else in all creation, will be able to separate us from the love of God that is in Christ Jesus our Lord." (Romans 8:38-39)

Amid the many issues involved in suicide, it is good for us to stay focused on the single truth that echoes throughout this chapter and the whole of Scripture. God accepts and loves us because of Jesus, and not even death, no matter what kind of death, can separate us from Him.

I have had the sad privilege of walking alongside many families who have experienced the pain of suicide. I have talked with individuals who have struggled with the despair that can eventually cause him or her to choose suicide as their option, and the loved ones left reeling with pain, grief, and woundedness when that option was chosen.

I had a friend who had been through terrible abuse as a child. By the time I knew him, he was a businessman with young children and a lovely wife. He was a godly man. On a particular Sunday, he and I had greeted each other with a hug and small talk for a brief time. A few days into the next week, I received a call from his wife who said he had been found by the police, having taken his life. Over the next days, weeks and months our church community surrounded her and her children with love and care. Over the years, I have learned that being in another's pain with them involves "being all there." God uses theory and practice, but God uses me and God uses you. And He wants me to be available, recognizing that He is the one who gives me wisdom and strength.

Yet another personal story comes from the family of a young teen, who following a week-end away with a youth group went up to his parent's bedroom and took his life. When our staff got the word, we headed for the church with streams of students pouring in until well past midnight grieving together, wanting to understand, wanting to hurt together.

Then there was the young teenage girl who took her life at a park right across from her Dad's home. Following the funeral, we provided a reception for family and friends and it was amazing that the teens who came felt at home in our church just wanting to be together.

My friend was a Pastor. Due to many difficulties in his life, including major physical disabilities, he went into that long dark emotional tunnel and did not come out. His brother, who preached at his funeral, during the message, looked at his watch as though he were God welcoming him home to Heaven and said "Hmm, you arrived a little early, didn't you?"

For someone who experiences the complicated grief of suicide, their need for loving care is perhaps even greater than through death by some other means.

As a God of hope, He offers that hope to us. He wants to fill us up with that hope. But I think sometimes we don't trust in Him, and the hope that could overflow in our lives seeps out because we have so many holes in our empty bucket.

As I mentioned, the Bible never comments directly about the morality of suicide. But when suicide happens, there is something we can state with absolute surety: that our God is a God of mercy and compassion and because of Jesus, nothing can separate us from Him, from His love.

Sometimes I sit in my backyard surrounded by a fence and envision an ocean which is unending, beautiful, majestic, and powerful. On first glance, there are very few similarities. My yard is finite, the ocean seems infinite; the fence marks a boundary, the ocean seems boundary-less. The ocean symbol is a picture of God's care, His love, His desire and availability to heal and bring comfort. So whether you are the giver of care or the one in need of it, ponder your own fences and God's ocean and recognize your need for both.

In helping one who hurts, there are, of necessity, boundaries, those of the caregiver and those of the person in need. The boundaries of the caregiver must include personal space and time, expertise or lack thereof, responsibility "to" the other person while not being responsible "for" the other person to change their mind, heal their pain or shorten their grief. The griever's boundaries must include personal responsibility, degree of trust in the caregiver, how much or how little of their story they share and ultimately what they choose to do with the gift of care.

As we ponder the weighty issues of suicide and hopelessness and pain and suffering, an arena for conflict that can lead to hopelessness is that of the family. A marriage crisis can either tear a couple apart or bring them closer together. Christian marriages are just as vulnerable as those in the world. Issues in the family can be the silent force that drives either adults or children to the brink of hopeless thinking.

The Chinese symbol for crisis means danger or opportunity. When a crisis hits, big or small, you have the option of going down one path or another, choosing that dangerous path that leads you further apart or choosing that opportunity road that brings you closer together, regardless how bumpy and painful the working through part may be.

Chapter 19
END THINGS—WHAT'S REALLY IMPORTANT

"Are we who we are when we die or are we younger?"

19

It's hard now to remember what she looked like in her 70's, I gave all my photographs of her to Scott. I wonder what we look like in heaven. Are we who we are when we die or are we younger? Will I have long hair or the ugly hair I have now? Will I have my teeth back or maybe we don't even have bodies, maybe we're transformed into beings of energy and yet we know who other people are, it will all be so fantastik. I hope grandma looks like herself, but I hope I look different. Lorene is in her late 50's or early 60's. It's one of those "glamour shots" and she is very beautiful with a big smile. I hope she's there to meet me too. I hope everyone I love will be there to meet me. I haven't said anything about my father and I should because I forgave him of everything a long time ago. I don't know if he made it to heaven but if he is then I guess it would be good to see him too. Maybe we could talk about the love he used to have for us before he got to be so bad. If that's the kind of love he has now, and must because only love can exist in heaven, then I would welcome seeing him too. He's probably there. I've heard so many times that our salvation doesn't have anything to do with good works but is our beliefs only, our faith that saves us to eternity. I know he believed, maybe he embraced it in the end, he had an easy death too as has everyone I know

When we have faced the pain of the death of suicide, we realize what a gift is the gift of time, the here and now. It is precious.

Having been involved in Caring Ministry for many years and having come to grips with the fact we all have a need for compassion, I am also aware of human limits of compassion. As I hear these words from the song, Mighty to Save: "Everyone needs compassion; the kindness of a Savior, love that never fails; let mercy fall on me; Everyone needs forgiveness; the kindness of a Savior," I recognize that my compassion has limits; that while I desire to have the kind of compassion that includes kindness, mercy, and forgiveness, I often fall short of extending that compassion to ALL who are around me. There are many in my life and in my ministry for whom showing compassion is easy. Others whom I encounter, not so much. They are the irregular people in my life who are difficult to care for, difficult to show compassion to. As I ponder the words of the song, I come to grips with the very real need and my inadequacy to even begin meeting such need. However, there is a God who can meet that need for compassion, kindness, mercy and forgiveness. Listen to this verse from Scripture:

> "Because of the Lord's great love we are not consumed, for His compassions never fail" Lamentations 3:22. His compassion does not have limits, it is ***compassion beyond measure.***

If we accept that we all have a need for compassion, how might that need be met? As you look in the mirror, would you describe the person looking back at you as a compassionate person? Even if the answer is yes, what might the limits of your compassion be? There are certain people in our lives or in the news, for that matter, who elicit compassion from us: the special needs child who runs his hardest in the race and crosses the finish line with a broad smile on his face; the brand new mommy whose husband has just been deployed; the baby who is the victim of parental abuse; the friend who recently lost his job; the couple who had to file for bankruptcy; the woman who was the victim of a carjacking; the young woman who was not invited to prom when all her friends were going.

What about these examples: the husband who decides to leave his wife; the classroom bully; the crisis-centered person; the talker in a meeting who has all the answers and won't let anyone else get a word in edgewise; the passive-aggressive person. What is our compassion level in some of these instances?

Understanding that not only do we all need compassion, but that God's compassion never fails, perhaps our *assignment* from God is more about sharing His compassion with others; letting them know of His love for them.

OK, so I'm left with knowing that you and I need compassion, and that God never runs out of that compassion. Since we know that God uses you and me to relate that compassion to others, what is the application for us? Perhaps it involves being in someone's pain with them and being all there. God wants me to listen to Him on the spot, to be available, to be used, and to be ministered to all at the same time. I can do nothing on my own without His using me; however, "I can do all things through Him who strengthens me." Philippians 4:13.

Chapter 20
WHAT IF?

"Therein lies the problem, there's nothing easy about waiting"

20

WHO'S DIED. MY DEATH HAS TO BE HARD, BUT MAYBE IF I WAITED FOR GOD'S TIMING IT WOULD BE EASY. THEREIN LIES THE PROBLEM, THERE'S NOTHING EASY ABOUT THE WAITING. SO REALLY, I'M THE ONE WHO'S MAKING DEATH SO HARD, MY CHOICE. 6 HOURS NOW, NERVES ARE TURNING INTO FEAR. 5 1/2 HOURS, MORE FEAR. ANOTHER REASON PEOPLE DON'T KNOW ABOUT IS THAT NOW THAT LORENE IS GONE I DON'T HAVE ANY WAY TO GET TO DOCTOR'S APPOINTMENTS OR THE STORE OR ANYWHERE. I COULD USE ACCESS-A-RIDE ONCE I SENT IN FOR THE CARD BUT THE PROBLEM IS THAT AN OXYGEN CYLINDER ONLY LASTS 1 1/2 HOURS OR LESS AND THERE'S NO WAY TO CARRY EXTRA TANKS ON THE RIDE. I REALLY AM STUCK HERE WITH NO WAY TO GO ANYWHERE, I SUPPOSE UNCLE WALT WOULDN'T MIND TAKING ME TO THE DOCTOR BUT THEN HOW WOULD I MAKE 5 APPOINTMENTS IN A MONTH TO GET MY TEETH FIXED AND THEY REALLY NEED TO BE FIXED. THAT POINT DOESN'T MATTER BECAUSE I DON'T HAVE THE $5000.00 TO GET THEM TAKEN CARE OF ANYWAY. BUT, EVEN TO GO TO 7-11 IT COSTS $6.00, $8.00 TO KING SOOPERS, MORE IF THEY HAVE TO WAIT AWHILE, THAT KIND OF CASH ADDS UP AND I CAN'T AFFORD IT. LORENE WAS MY LIFELINE AND I REALLY NEVER CONSIDERED HER BEING GONE, SHE WAS ALWAYS SO HEALTHY UNTIL SHE GOT CANCER. I WAS CONVINCED THAT I WOULD DIE BEFORE HER, THAT'S WHY SHE WAS THE BENEFICIARY OF MY LIFE INSURANCE BEFORE I CHANGED IT TO UNCLE WALT. NO ONE KNOWS WHAT ITS LIKE TO BE STUCK IN THIS APARTMENT DAY AFTER DAY WITH ONLY THE T.V. AS COMPANY.

Not only do we all need compassion, we all need a safe place. I've been pondering my safe place these past few days and wondering if my safe place is in reality a place or a person? I took a long walk the other night, winding up at the cemetery where my parents are both buried. I spent some quiet time sitting by their graves, thinking, reflecting, and praying. Some of you may be more inclined to visit the graves of loved ones than I am. That was an unusual decision for me. I'm not one who goes back to the cemetery typically on Memorial Day, birthdays, anniversaries. I know that my parents are with Jesus, and though right after my Mom's death I found her grave a place of comfort, I have not chosen to make that stop for a long time. Why the other night? Why did I wind up there? I'm not sure that is a question easily answered except to say, I needed to do some reflecting and pray in a safe place.

What will today hold for you? Perhaps you went to bed last night with a heavy heart or a tired body or a confused mind. You may have slept fitfully and awakened feeling sluggish, unrested, hurried and harried, and dreading this day. Will it be a repeat of yesterday? Might you have some of the same disagreements you had yesterday? Are the stressors in your life going to increase rather than decrease with the added pressures of today?

God is a God of new beginnings. God is a God of love. God is the Redeemer. The God of love reminds us that His love is ever new and eternal. The Redeemer God shows us that God can and does redeem our pain. He invades our life with people and events that direct us; He graces us with wisdom and direction. What will today hold for you? It is a new day that God has made.

Chapter 21
HOPE

"There are so many things I would do
differently if I could only go back..."

21

4 HOURS AND I'M VERY TIRED I WISH TIME WASN'T GOING BY SO FAST. THERE ARE SO MANY THINGS I WOULD DO DIFFERENTLY IF I COULD ONLY GO BACK AND CHANGE HAVING A HEART ATTACK AND GETTING SO SICK WITH COPD. I AM SUCH A DIFFERENT PERSON NOW, SO MUCH CLOSER TO GOD. I SPENT SO MUCH OF MY LIFE RUNNING AWAY FROM MY PAIN AND PROBLEMS INSTEAD OF FACING IT ALL AND ASKING GOD TO HELP ME. SO MUCH TIME SPENT DRINKING TO EXCESS AND USING DRUGS. I NEVER WAS THE BEST THAT I COULD BE BECAUSE OF THAT, I WOULD CHANGE EVERYTHING IF I COULD ONLY BE WELL AND NOT NEED OXYGEN. I HAVE WANTED TO GO TO CHURCH FOR A LONG TIME BUT WASN'T ABLE TO. I SHOULD HAVE JOINED A CHURCH SO MANY YEARS AGO. BUT WHAT GOOD DOES IT DO TO THINK OF ALL THE "WHAT IFS" NOW? IT DOESN'T CHANGE WHAT I HAVE TO DO. THERE IS JUST NO WAY FOR ME TO SURVIVE THIS. GOING TO HEAVEN IS THE ONLY WAY TO MAKE IT ALL BETTER. I HOPE SOMEONE WILL UNDERSTAND THAT THIS ISN'T WHAT I WANT TO DO, IT'S WHAT I NEED TO DO. GOD HAS BEEN SO FAITHFUL TO ME IN THIS LIFE, HE HAS ALWAYS GIVEN ME SO MUCH EVEN THOUGH I DIDN'T DESERVE ANY OF IT. BUT I TOOK IT ALL FOR GRANTED BEFORE AND THREW A LOT OF THE GIFTS AWAY. I'M GLAD I LIVED LONG ENOUGH TO TRULY BE ABLE TO SEE THE THINGS I'VE DONE WRONG IN LIFE AND ASKED GOD TO FORGIVE ME FOR. AND I KNOW THAT I'M FORGIVEN SAVE THE FINAL THING I MUST DO.

My "Top Eleven" To Do's in ministering to those who are hurting.

1. Being in someone's pain with them involves being all there. God uses theory and practice, but God uses me and God uses you. God wants me to listen to Him on the spot: to be available, to be used, and to be ministered to all at the same time. I can do nothing on my own without His using me; however, "I can do all things through Him who strengthens me." (Philippians 4:13)

2. I need to respect the dignity of those who come through my doors or over my phone line for help, even those who may be difficult or may push my buttons. I need to have a spirit of discernment, and to be non-judgmental. I may not agree with them, but they are still in pain and in need of a listener.

3. It is important to have a view from another's eyes. While a baby's baptism may be for those involved a joyous occasion, there may be those in attendance for whom it is extremely painful, those struggling with their singleness or their infertility, those who would love to be, but never will be, parents or grandparents.

4. As much as I might wish it, I cannot take away another's pain, nor can I fix the problem, but I can help to bear the burdens of that one. This is what I am called to do, "Bear one another's burdens and thus fulfill the law of Christ." (Galatians 6:2)

5. I have learned to listen, and that to give my example or to tell my story, which may at the time seem relevant to me, may actually be a deterrent. What really matters is their story and their need to tell it, and to have someone really listen so they can tell it often.

6. Silence is precious; words need to be guarded carefully. Sometimes incessant talking and inappropriate humor can be

an irritant. Whose needs am I meeting, mine or the one for whom I am caring?

7. Sometimes I need to be bold in giving care. I need to have the freedom to ask the delicate, uncomfortable questions. Perhaps God will use me to ask, "Are you afraid?" "Are you struggling?" "Was it hurtful?"

8. I don't know everything, and therefore, I strongly believe in the value and beauty of team and corporate wisdom. I don't always have to have an answer or give my opinion. Sometimes the greatest care I can give is to find out what wisdom someone else might have to share in a particular situation

9. There is beauty in "rejoice with those who rejoice; mourn with those who mourn". Romans 12:15. God uses the comfort I have received to comfort another.

10. Grief takes as long as it takes, is a process rather than a destination, and I dare not put another on my time table for healing.

11. The death bed is a very holy place for the believer but for the one who doesn't have the assurance of going to be with Jesus, it may be terrifying for the dying person or their family. If we are privileged to be with them, our being with them in that moment is Jesus being with them while holding their hand.

Chapter 22
WHAT IS MOST IMPORTANT?

"Like I said before, I never said this was the right
thing to do. Just a Little While and There Will Be Rest."

22

I'VE ASKED HIM SO MANY TIMES TO FORGIVE ME FOR IT AND NOT TO HOLD IT AGAINST ME. I CAN ONLY HOPE THAT HE WILL. I DON'T BLAME GOD FOR ANYTHING THAT'S GOING ON NOW. LIKE IT OR NOT, I BROUGHT THIS ALL ON MYSELF BY BAD LIFE DECISIONS OR JUST NOT MAKING GOOD ONES. BUT I HOPE HE UNDERSTANDS HOW I FEEL, THAT THERE'S ONLY ONE WAY OUT OF THIS HELL I FIND MYSELF IN. I HOPE HE FACTORS THAT INTO JUDGING FOR CHOOSING MY OWN WILL OVER HIS. I FEEL SO BAD ABOUT IT. LIKE I SAID BEFORE, I NEVER SAID THIS WAS THE RIGHT THING TO DO. 3 1/2 HOURS AND I'M SO TIRED THAT I'M FALLING ASLEEP IN THE CHAIR. JUST A LITTLE WHILE AND THERE WILL BE REST. WHAT AM I THE MOST AFRAID OF AT THIS MOMENT? THAT 3:30 WILL COME AND I'LL PROCRASTINATE UNTIL IT'S TOO LATE AGAIN. AFTER THAT IT'S THE ACTUAL LETTING GO. I'M SOMEWHAT AFRAID OF HOW IT WILL BE, I GUESS LIKE BEING CHOKED TO DEATH, I CAN ONLY HOPE THAT IT'S FAST. I'M NOT AFRAID OF ACTUALLY DYING, ONLY WHAT I HAVE TO GO THROUGH TO GET TO THAT POINT. IF I KEEP MY MIND ON THE LIGHT THAT WILL COME FLOODING IN AND GRANDMA AND LORENE COMING TO MEET ME. SCOTT THINKS THAT AN ANGEL COMES FOR US TO MEET JESUS IN THE AIR AND THAT JESUS TAKES US TO A PLACE HE HAS PREPARED FOR US. BUT I LIKE TO THINK IT WILL BE GRANDMA TO COME TO MEET ME. IF I SAW AN ANGEL I MIGHT BE AFRAID BUT WHEN I SEE GRANDMA I'LL KNOW THAT EVERYTHIN

New Beginnings

Do not ever forget; God uses programs, training and experience; but more importantly, God uses you in caring for another; your servant heart, your uniqueness, guided by His Spirit. God uses you. As He chooses to use us, He also equips us as grace-givers. It is a privilege to be making decisions based upon what is best for the other.

"Do nothing out of selfish ambition or vain conceit, but in humility consider others better than yourselves. Each of you should look not only to his own interests, but also to the interests of others." Philippians 2:3.

Chapter 23
GOD EMPOWERS

*"I wish I was there already but I have to
get through the really hard part first."*

23

IS ALRIGHT. I WISH I WAS THERE ALREADY BUT I
HAVE TO GET THROUGH THE REALLY HARD PART FIRST.
IT IS SO IMPORTANT THAT THIS WORK, I JUST ASKED
GOD TO PLEASE NOT HINDER ME AND TO LET ME GO
BECAUSE I CAN'T BE ANY STRONGER. I CAN'T ASK HIM
TO HELP ME, BUT I DON'T WANT TO WIND UP STILL
ALIVE AT THE END OF IT. I JUST COULDN'T TAKE THAT,
NOT TO MENTION THAT IF I'M STILL ALIVE WHEN THEY
CUT ME DOWN THEY'LL PROBABLY MAKE ME GO TO A
HOSPITAL. THAT WOULD JUST BE ANOTHER SET OF PROBLEMS
IT JUST HAS TO WORK. BUT I'VE NEVER HEARD OF
ANYONE WHO HANGED THEMSELF THAT WEREN'T
SUCCESSFUL. I WILL JUST GO WITH THE ASSUMPTION
THAT IT WILL WORK JUST FINE. 2 1/2 HOURS, IT WILL
BE HERE SOON. WHAT A JOY TO NOT HAVE TO SPEND ONE
MORE ENDLESS DAY IN THIS AWFUL PLACE. I KEEP WANTING
TO ASK THE LORD FOR COURAGE, BUT I CAN'T ASK FOR HELP
TO DO THE WRONG THING. I HAVE TO FIND THE STRENGTH
IN ME SOMEWHERE DOWN DEEP AND BRING IT TO THE
SURFACE. I HAVE THE RESOLVE, EVERYTIME THE THOUGHT
CREEPS IN TO WAIT I SAY NO - TOMORROW WILL BE THE
SAME AS TODAY ONLY WORSE BECAUSE I'LL HAVE TO TRY
TO DO THE LAUNDRY AND TAKE ANOTHER SHOWER. I'M
HARDLY BREATHING WELL ENOUGH TO GO UP TO THE
BALCONY. HOW FREE I WILL FEEL WHEN I TAKE OFF
THE PORTABLE OXYGEN TO NEVER HAVE TO NEED IT
AGAIN. I TRUST SOMEONE WILL BRING THE PORTABLE BACK
DOWN AND PUT IT IN FRONT OF MY DOOR. I DECIDED

While accepting that God is a God of new beginnings, what if everything appears the same in your life:

- You are still out of work.
- Singleness is still an issue you struggle with.
- Your husband told you during the holidays that he did not want to be married to you anymore.
- You and your wife made it through another holiday, barely holding it together without fighting in front of the kids.
- You are still holding on to the anger you felt before the turn of the calendar year.
- Your teenage son is still rebellious.
- Your hearing is still diminishing.
- The hip replacement surgery is still looming.
- You still have to help your aging parent see that they need to move out of their home.
- You are still struggling with infertility.
- Finances are still tight; in fact, the situation is worse because you charged Christmas gifts to your credit card.

Chapter 24
WE CAN'T DO IT ON OUR OWN

*"One thing I forgot to mention before
but I think I might be dying soon anyway."*

24

LOCK THE DOOR AND TAKE MY KEYS BECAUSE I LEFT MY PIN IN A NOTE TO UNCLE WALT. HE CAN GET THE KEYS FROM THE POLICE TO GET INTO THE APARTMENT. THERE'S NO HURRY FOR HIM TO GET OVER HERE AND TAKE CARE OF ANYTHING. ALL HE HAS TO DO IS CALL THE MANAGER AND LET HIM KNOW THAT HE'LL BE OVER EVENTUALLY. THEY WON'T CUT THE POWER AND PHONE UNTIL THE MIDDLE OF NEXT MONTH AND IT DOESN'T MATTER THAT THE RENT WON'T BE PAID ON SEPT. 1ST. THEY HAVE TO LET HIM GET THINGS OUT OF HERE REGARDLESS. MAYBE HE'LL JUST LEAVE IT TO THEM TO DO. IT DOESN'T MATTER EITHER WAY HE'LL HAVE THE TIME TO DEAL WITH IT. 2 HOURS LEFT, IT'S GOING BY SO FAST. ALL I HAVE TO DO IS PUT ON MY SHOES, GET THE ROPE, PUT ON THE PORTABLE, LOCK THE DOOR AND CLIMB THE STAIRS. I HOPE NO ONE COMES OUT, BUT THEN, WHAT NORMAL PERSON WOULD BE OUT AT 3:30 AM.? NO ONE CAN ACCUSE ME OF BEING VAIN BECAUSE I'M WEARING THE SAME CLOTHES I HAD ON YESTERDAY AND I NEED ANOTHER SHOWER. I SMELL LIKE SMOKE SINCE I SMOKED A WHOLE PACK TONIGHT. ONE THING I FORGOT TO MENTION BEFORE BUT I THINK I MIGHT BE DYING SOON ANYWAY. I'M UP TO 8 ON MY OXYGEN NOW WHICH IS WHY I'M HAVING SO MUCH PROBLEM WITH MY SINUSES. I DON'T WANT TO DIE LAYING IN A BED GASPING FOR AIR. I CAN'T COMPLAIN ABOUT THAT BECAUSE I JUST WOULDN'T GIVE UP THE CIGARETTES. THE BREATHING

It is into this life that Jesus came, for you and for me. He came to make all things new, not to take us out of our difficulties and joblessness and pain and suffering but in the midst of those things that are still happening in our lives, to give us a new beginning while in the midst of it all. Right here, right now.

He wants to give us fresh eyes, an alternative perspective in our recognition that He is with us; that He will never leave us nor forsake us; that "In this world you will have suffering; but be of good cheer, for I have overcome the world." John 16:33. He wants us to understand that He is a redeeming God and can bring wholeness and newness out of broken pieces. I definitely don't have it all figured out. I struggle, too. I deal with disappointments as well. I definitely don't always understand God's ways.

I hurt like you, but I am confident of this: "The steadfast love of the Lord never ceases; His mercies are new every morning, great is His faithfulness." Lamentations 3:22-23. God is indeed a God of new beginnings.

Chapter 25
THE FINAL CHAPTER

25

MEDICATIONS DON'T WORK TOO WELL ANYMORE. THE MACHINE ONLY GOES UP TO 10 AND THE PORTABLE IS MAXED AT 8. IF I HAD TO GO UP AGAIN I WOULDN'T EVER BE ABLE TO LEAVE THE APARTMENT. WHEN THIS ALL STARTED IN 2006 I WAS AT A LEVEL 4 AND I WAS USING THE PULSED REGULATOR WHICH ALLOWS 8 HOURS ON A TANK AS LITTLE AS 6 MONTHS AGO. I JUST RAISED IT FROM A 6 TO A 7 BACK IN MAY. SO I DON'T THINK IT WILL BE LONG BEFORE THE EMPHYSEMA WOULD CAUSE MY DEATH. I'M TRYING TO RATIONALIZE DYING LIKE SOMEHOW IT MAKES IT LESS WRONG SINCE MY LUNGS HAVE GOTTEN SO MUCH WORSE. BUT I CAN'T, IT'S STILL WRONG. YES, I HAVE BROUGHT THIS ALL ON MYSELF, NO ONE ELSE IS TO BLAME. IT'S NOT GOD'S FAULT THAT I'VE CONTINUED TO SMOKE. I HAD EVERY INTENTION OF QUITTING AGAIN BUT MAYBE UNDERNEATH IT ALL I'M JUST COMPLETELY SELF-DESTRUCTIVE, I KNOW THAT I DON'T LOVE MYSELF VERY MUCH OR I WOULDN'T HAVE LET MY LIFE GET INTO THIS HUGE MESS. EVERYTHING SEEMS TOO LITTLE TOO LATE. IT'S ALL NEITHER HERE NOR THERE NOW AND I DON'T WANT TO LEAVE FEELING BAD ABOUT MYSELF. 1 1/2 HOURS AND 1/2 HOUR AND I'LL BE GONE. THERE'S NO POINT IN WRITING ANYMORE, I HAVE TO GET READY. IT'S ALMOST TIME. GOOD-BYE LIFE-HELLO GRANDMA, I'LL BE THERE SOON.

Memorial Service for Kathy
August 29, 2012

Military Honors

All Veteran's Tribute

Prayer: "Father, we come today to celebrate the life of Kathryn Louise MacQueen. We ask that you help us to grieve but not as those who have no hope. Help us to understand the hope of Heaven and the comfort of your Spirit. We ask because of Jesus. Amen."

Scripture: Psalms 139:7-18

"Where can I go from your Spirit? If I go up to the heavens, you are there; if I make my bed in the depths, you are there. If I rise on the wings of the dawn, if I settle on the far side of the sea, even there your hand will guide me, your right hand will hold me fast.

If I say, "Surely, the darkness will hide me and the light become night around me," even the darkness will not be dark to you; the night will shine like the day, for darkness is as light to you.

For you created my inmost being; you knit me together in my mother's womb. I praise you because I am fearfully and wonderfully made, your works are wonderful, I know that full well. My frame was not hidden from you when I was made in the secret place. When I was woven together in the depths of the earth, your eyes saw my unformed body.

All the days ordained for me were written in your book before one of them came to be. How precious to me are your thoughts, O God. How vast is the sum of them. Were I to count them, they would outnumber the grains of sand. When I awake, I am still with you."

Kathy's life:

Birth: Kathy was born on July 28, 1958.

Death: Kathy died on August 21, 2012.

Military: Perhaps Kathy's time serving in our military in Spain were some of the happiest days of her life.

Career: It was during her military service that she developed the skill of becoming a welder, which led to her brief career at Martin Marietta.

Struggles: Kathy's life was difficult—none of us would dispute that. She suffered long and hard. Kathy did not place blame nor did she shirk the responsibility that she felt was hers in many of these struggles. But Kathy was a very loving person and really loved her family—especially Grandma Lydia. In fact, her last words were filled with her desire to join Grandma and Lorene and Jesus in Heaven. Kathy had a vision of Heaven that was beautiful. Her own Words, she pictured heaven as a place where God would use each of us in the ways in which he has gifted us. She even pictured that Grandma might be working with children. She had asked God to forgive her for taking her life, and she was very confident in his love for her and his mercy toward her. As Gene shares The Lord's Prayer—may it be our heart's prayer.

"The Lord's Prayer" sung by Gene Roberts

Benediction: "Father, we acknowledge that you are a Holy, Merciful God—and we now commend to you Kathryn Louise MacQueen. Thank you for her life and thank you for the assurance that she is with you. Thank you for your love and your faithfulness. Now, as we leave this place, may our hearts be more in tune with you and with others in need of your love and our loving touch. In Jesus' loving, powerful, name—the name above any other. Amen."

Chapter 26
THE JOURNAL COMPLETE

26

3:30 A.M,
08/21/12
THE END

EPILOGUE

A fellow resident of the apartment complex where Kathy had been living found Kathy. 911 was called, but by the time they arrived and got her down, reviving her was not possible. As Kathy planned and stated in her journal, she had pinned a note to her shirt to call her uncle Walt when she was found, including his phone number. That call triggered other calls to relatives and friends. My husband Ken, another of Kathy's uncles and Walt's brother, received the call from Walt that morning. Ken then called me. He also called Kathy's mother who offered to cover any outstanding expenses.

Kathy's funeral service was held at Fort Logan National Cemetery just west of Denver, Colorado. Since Kathy was an honorably discharged veteran of the United States Air Force, she was given full military honors including a 21-gun salute. Her cremated remains have been placed in a cemetery niche at Fort Logan National Cemetery.

Reading through Kathy's journal numerous times does not make the circumstances of her death or the pain of her life easier to cope with, but we are grateful for the Hope of Heaven knowing that Kathy is with Jesus. Whether those reading this book are ones who are hurting or caregivers coming alongside of the hurting, my desire is that some will be helped by Kathy's story.

ABOUT THE AUTHOR

 Barbara Roberts has years of experience, walking beside individuals and families—many who struggle with pain and loss and despair. She is the Director of Caring Ministry at Cherry Creek Presbyterian Church. She and her husband, Ken, live in the Denver area.

She is the author of *Helping Those Who Hurt: A Handbook for Caring and Crisis.*